THE FIRST COWBOYS
AND THOSE
WHO FOLLOWED

THE FIRST

by

CHARLES ZURHORST

COWBOYS AND THOSE WHO FOLLOWED

ABELARD-SCHUMAN
New York | London
An Intext *Publisher*

FOR
Susie,
Craig,
AND
Chuck

Copyright © 1973 by Charles Zurhorst

All rights reserved. No part of this book may be reprinted, or reproduced or utilized in any form or by any electronic, mechanical or other means, now known or hereafter invented, including photocopying and recording, or in any information storage and retrieval system, without permission in writing from the Publisher.

Abelard-Schuman Ltd., 257 Park Avenue South, New York, N.Y. 10010

Published on the same day in Canada by Longman Canada Limited.
Printed in the United States of America

NEW YORK	LONDON
Abelard-Schuman	Abelard-Schuman
Limited	Limited
257 Park Avenue So.	450 Edgware Road, London W21EG
10010	and
	24 Market Square, Aylesbury, Bucks.

Library of Congress Cataloging in Publication Data

Zurhorst, Charles.
    The first cowboys and those who followed.
      Bibliography: p.
      1. Cowboys.   I. Title.
F596.Z87   978   72–9545
ISBN 0–200–04001–4

CONTENTS

PART ONE

The First Cowboys

What Is a Cowboy?	3
Mystery of the Origin	9
By Error or Design	14
Samuel Munro, Woodsrunner	20
Turmoil on the Hudson	25
Westward Went the Rebels	31
On to Texas	36
Point 'Em North	41
Broader Horizons	46

PART
TWO

Those Who Followed

A Degree of Recognition	53
Cowboy Trailblazers	57
Frontier Cowboy Businessmen	67
Frontier Cowboy Ranchers	74
Frontier Cowboys Who Became Politicians	82
Frontier Cowboys Who Became Lawmen	88
Frontier Cowboys of the Arts	94
Transitional Frontier Cowboys	99
Rodeos and Rodeo Cowboys	104
Other Great Westerners	130
Bibliography	143
Index	147

LIST OF ILLUSTRATIONS

The cowboy of art, literature, films and television	5
The pre-Revolution cowboy of Dutchess County, New York	15
The Texas cowboy of the 1820's	37
The Texas cowboy of the trail drive era	43
Robert Simpson Ford	59
Charles Goodnight	61
Conrad Kohrs	62
Oliver Loving	63
Daniel Waggoner	65
Charles F. Coffee	68
James Taylor Craig	69
James K. Hitch	70
Tom Jones	71
Morell Case Keith	72
G. E. Lemmon	73
Samuel Burk Burnett	75
James Henry Cook	76
Myron D. Jeffers	77
James Philip	79
Daniel Clay Wheeler	81
Will C. Barnes	83
Charles E. Collins	84
James C. Dahlman	85

John Benjamin Kendrick	86
Charles Francis Colcord	89
John W. Goodall	90
Burton C. "Cap" Mossman	91
George C. Ruffner	92
John Marcellus "Tex" Moore	95
Eugene Manlove Rhodes	96
Charles Russell	97
William F. "Buffalo Bill" Cody	100
Tom Mix	101
Charles Harland Tompkins	102
Will Rogers	103
Doff Aber	106
Lewis Edward Bowman	107
Clyde Burk	109
Chester Byers	110
Lee R. Caldwell	111
Paul Carney	113
Bob Crosby	114
Edwin Louis Curtis	115
George "Kid" Fletcher	116
Pete Knight	117
William E. "Bill" Linderman	119
Eddie McCarty	120
Jake McClure	121
Lee Robinson	123
Hugh Strickland	125
William Leonard Stroud	126
Fritz Truan	128
Oral Harris Zumwalt	129

PREFACE

This is the first book ever to reveal the origin of the American cowboy, and this fact alone deserves some word of explanation.

The discovery of the origin of the American cowboy was completely by accident—a classic case of serendipity. I doubt that anyone could begin with the modern cowboy and trace him back step by step to his beginning. There are too many dead ends going in that direction.

However, in 1951, my wife, Susie, and I were doing research in Dutchess County, New York, which involved working forward from the end of the seventeenth century to the middle of the nineteenth century. It was this combination of the area we were studying and the direction in which we were developing our research that caused the continuing intrusion of the unrelated word "cowboy" to form a pattern.

Intrigued by this implausible pattern, later we turned our attention to the cowboy as such, and made the study of him our prime research target. It has continued since then to the time of the writing of this book.

In that research there are many persons to be thanked for their assistance. However, particular thanks should go to the late Rutherfoord Goodwin, researcher, curator, and historian at Colonial Williamsburg, Virginia. His guidance and assistance, based on his previous associations with the Philipse Castle restoration in New York, were invaluable.

Special thanks, too, should go to Michael Cohn, Curator of the Brooklyn, New York, Children's Museum, and to his wife, Susan, for their archeological confirmation of the historical research, and for providing a home at the Brooklyn Children's Museum for the relics uncovered to date at the birthplace of the American cowboy, now identified as New York State Archeological Site CLo 1–3.

In addition, sincere thanks should go to the Texas State Library Archives Division, the Texas State Historical Survey Committee, and Mrs. Lu Osborn at the National Cowboy Hall of Fame in Oklahoma City, Oklahoma.

Also thanks to Mrs. Amy VerNooy, of the Adriance Memorial Library in Poughkeepsie, New York, for all the research she did on her own as a gesture of her interest in both Dutchess County and the American cowboy.

Many who helped became personal friends, and for this we are the most thankful.

CHARLES ZURHORST

Litchfield, Connecticut

PART
ONE

THE FIRST COWBOYS

WHAT IS A COWBOY?

According to one old-timer, "A cowboy is a carefree man with a lot of guts, a super sense of justice, and a horse that is worth more than he is."

According to another, "A cowboy is a fellow who is dedicated to one thing—being a cowboy. I have seen a lot of different types of men from a lot of different states become cowboys. But, once they become cowboys, they will never admit to being anything else."

Cowboys have been called symbols of eternal youth, symbols of adventure, symbols of independence, and the most colorful figures in American folklore.

"Ideally," according to Joe B. Frantz and Julian Ernest Choate, Jr., in their book, *The American Cowboy*, [he] was a superb horseman, which as a fact he was; an expert of the fast draw and the use of a Colt revolver, which he might have been; a dead shot with a Winchester; brave beyond question; always on the side of justice, even if that justice be a bit stern at times; the defender of virtuous women; the implacable foe of the Indian; and a man to whom honor and integrity came naturally."

Substantiating this definition is a contemporary cowboy joke, which obviously has two versions. It has to do with a cowboy playing a sentimental tune on a piano in a Western saloon. While he is playing, a gunslinger enters through the swinging doors, carefully eyes the room and everybody in it, and then saunters arrogantly over to the piano player.

Without moving his thumbs from his holster belt and scarcely moving his lips, the gunslinger mutters to the cowboy, "I came here to drink and when I drink I don't want no piano playing."

The cowboy pays no attention and, not missing a note, continues as though he were alone in the saloon.

With this, the gunslinger whips out his six-shooter, shoots a cuff link out of one of the cowboy's sleeves, and again mutters, "I said when I drink, I don't want no piano playing."

The cowboy still ignores him and continues with the tune.

The gunslinger then shoots the cuff link out of the cowboy's other sleeve, but still gets no reaction from him.

At this point, the bartender catches the gunslinger's eye, and beckons him to the bar. Leaning across, he whispers, "My friend, I don't like to interfere, but I do have one suggestion to make."

The gunslinger looks quizzical and the bartender continues, "I would suggest that you leave here for a couple of minutes, go down the street to the general store, and put a heavy coating of lard on that gun of yours."

"Why the hell should I do that?" the gunslinger asks.

"Because," replies the bartender, "when that cowboy finishes the song he is dedicating to his mother, he's going to take that gun of yours and shove it right up your nose."

Additional confirmation of the fact that the cowboy thinks of himself as a special kind of man is the recipe he claims is his favorite recipe for making coffee. It goes like this: Take one pound of coffee, wet it well with one cup of water, and boil it over an open fire for thirty minutes. At the end of this time, drop a horseshoe into it. If the horseshoe sinks, add more coffee.

To sum up the image of the American cowboy as seen by himself and the public, little more is needed than the saloon anecdote and the coffee recipe.

He is rugged (who else could drink that kind of coffee?), he is tender (who else would dedicate a song on a barroom piano to his mother?), he is an outdoorsman (his recipe calls for an open fire), his constant

companion is his horse (otherwise his coffee-making technique might call for a rock instead of a horseshoe), and he is dedicated to justice (note what he will doubtless do with the gunslinger's gun).

No figure in American history or American folklore has ever enjoyed a better image. And basically there was, and is, a sound foundation for this.

Working cowboys, in the heyday of ranching, had to be of a certain type or they would not have chosen to be cowboys in the first place. The same, to a slightly lesser degree, holds true today. Ruggedness, independence, tenderness, and a sense of justice are all necessary characteristics of this type.

On a range, life can be hard and demanding, and lonesome. It takes a good man to face it and endure it. And, if a young calf strays, it takes a tender man to seek it out, calm it, handle it, and return it to its mother.

As for justice, it is a clearly defined word on any range, for range life has no room for shades of good and bad, right and wrong. A man is a crook or he is honest. He is lazy or he is a good worker. Living and working are too closely related for any other interpretation.

Similarly, water in a spring hole can never be "just a little bit poisoned." It is either fit to drink or not fit to drink. And a cut line fence is a cut line fence, no matter how few head of cattle manage to get through before it is repaired.

So the foundation for the image is there and existed long before the days of the Wild West, long before the days of Cameron's Cowboys in Texas in the 1830's, even long before the days of the American Revolution. But its glamorization over the years has, nevertheless, made it more of an image than a reality.

Motion pictures, radio series, television series, novels, dime novels, and comic books have all contributed to this glamorization. They have been responsible for the American cowboy's unchallenged role as this nation's favorite and most famous folk hero, and they should not be criticized for this. What they have done might well be interpreted in the long run as rendering justice to a deserving figure.

Until as recently as 1870, the reputation of the cowboy was not enviable, and no one had even considered giving him an ideal image. But in 1870 articles and paperbacks, forerunners of the dime novel, were written by a Ned Buntline, a pseudonym for Edward Zane Carroll Judson, a newspaper feature writer who had been unsuccessfully lynched for a murder, had led a mob in the New York Astor Place riot, and then gone west seeking more adventure.

The real-life hero of his stories, although not as a cowboy, was William Frederick Cody, better remembered as Buffalo Bill. Buntline had bumped into him accidentally, chatted with him, and found enough basic material on which he could elaborate in his Buffalo Bill yarns.

Dime novels, novels, and stories in *Scribner's Monthly* magazine, with the West as their background and the cowboy as their hero, then began appearing. All seemed to follow the same pattern in building an image for the cowboy.

By 1895 their propaganda had begun to take hold. In his book *Ten Years a Cowboy,* published in 1895, C. C. Post stated: "Formerly the man who shouted loudest, galloped hardest, and was quickest in drawing his 'gun,' was considered the most dashing cow-boy; if he had come up on the Texas trail, and had failed to kill his man, he was held to have wasted his opportunities. But times are changing; it is only in the South —for instance, Arizona—where the term cow-boy is equivalent to desperado."

Regardless, there did exist that basic element of truth underlying the image.

Buffalo Bill, although an uneducated farmboy from Iowa who had served as a Union soldier before he turned buffalo hunter and scout, was said to have been always a gallant gentleman, even before he became famous.

Wild Bill Hickok, six feet, two inches tall, stood with a look of authority. He had a broad chest, small waist, muscular arms and legs, and obviously was capable of handling problem situations. But his eyes were as tender and gentle-appearing as those of a woman in love. And although he is credited with having shot and killed more than one hundred men, it is claimed that not one fell except in the interpretation of the word justice.

A third example is the famed cowboy-turned-marshal, Wyatt Earp. Tall, slender, and strong, Earp was also polite and soft-spoken. Perhaps more than any other marshal in history, he managed to outwit and "talk in" criminals without resorting to gunplay.

These are the facts on which the cowboy's image was founded, first by Buntline with his Buffalo Bill stories, then by other writers, including Charles Siringo, Emerson Hough, Zane Grey, Owen Wister, and Clarence Mulford with his Hopalong Cassidy series.

The pattern stayed the same and continued when Hollywood expanded the cowboy's appeal with the help of actors like William S. Hart, Tom Mix, Buck Jones, Hoot Gibson, Gary Cooper, Joel McCrea, and John Wayne. Then came many radio series, still following the same image, and reaching new audiences, with the Lone Ranger and America's first singing show-business cowboy, Gene Autry. And television, not inclined to bypass good box office, played its contributing role through series like "Gunsmoke," "Bonanza," "High Chaparral," "Wyatt Earp," and "The Men from Shiloh."

But since 1870, and in all media, the image-building pattern has remained the same. The cowboy is rugged, polite, gentle, and dedicated to justice. Cowboys are always good guys. There are no bad cowboys. There are bad men, bad guys, bandits, desperados, robbers, and gunslingers, but never a bad cowboy, as such.

The artistically masterful cowboy illustrations by such painters as Charles Russell and Frederic Remington enhanced this image, and songs the cowboys sang added the finishing touch.

Since 1870, therefore, there has been ample reason why the cowboy's popularity remains unsurpassed.

He was everything most men have always wanted to be—independent. Stories of his escapades provided escape—escape into the person of this adventurous hero and into his world of excitement and justice.

And who could dislike a man who wanted his home to be in an area where deer and antelope played, where discouraging words were seldom heard, and where the skies were always sunny? This is what the cowboy asked for in one of his favorite songs, "Home on the Range."

Yet, with all the attention that the American cowboy has received in art, music, literature, movies, radio, and television, precious little is known of the man. Everyone knows *what* the cowboy is, but no one has ever bothered to find out *who* the cowboy is.

MYSTERY OF THE ORIGIN

In his Western classic, *The Story of the Cowboy,* Emerson Hough wrote, "Let us not ask whence the cowboy came, for that is a question immaterial and impossible of answer. Be sure he came from among those who had strong within them that savagery and love of freedom which springs so swiftly into life among strong natures when offered a brief exemption from the slavery of civilization."

Subsequent authors and historians seem to have shared Hough's opinion that the origin of the cowboy was a mystery that would never be solved, for few even tried. And those few who did try always ended in conflict with others, and often in conflict with themselves.

Merit Students' Encyclopedia explains the cowboy's origin in this fashion: "Cowboys were cattle herders. They were products of two cultures, the Anglo-Saxon from the eastern slopes of the Appalachians, who ran a few cows along the slopes and up valleys, and the Spanish-Mexican-Indian of the American Southwest, who ranged his cattle over thousands of semi-arid square miles, paying little attention to his herd except for twice-a-year roundups. These two cultures converged in Texas, where they blended into that unique American, the western cowboy."

An article in the Plainfield, New Jersey, *Courier News* of August 3, 1955, stated: "He was born an Easterner, rode a Moorish horse, took his ways from Mexico, and became a legend. His business title: American cowboy."

However, the same article went on to quote the National Geographic Society as saying the first cowboy came "from Ireland, from Spain, from backwoods Massachusetts, from tidewater Virginia."

Bruce Grant, in *The Cowboy Encyclopedia*, says, "The word 'cowboy' originated in Texas."

But the September 29, 1968, issue of the *New York Times,* in referring to an area in Westchester County, New York, stated: "To the south was a no-man's land (during the Revolutionary War) in which 'cowboys' ranged at will, stealing the horses and cattle of the residents. Tories or Tory sympathizers, they got their name from their practice of luring loyal Americans into traps in the brush by tinkling cowbells."

Ramon Adams, in his *Western Words—A Dictionary of the American West,* agrees with the *New York Times* on the time and place, but not on the reason the Westchester County marauders were called cowboys. He writes, "This word [cowboy] seems to have originated in Revolutionary days, when a group of Tory guerrillas roamed the region between the lines in Westchester County, New York, and called themselves by this name. I have never been able to discover why they gave themselves this name, since they had nothing to do with cows except for stealing a few."

Many other current dictionaries, encyclopedias, and histories identify the Revolutionary War cowboys as Tory marauders, raiders, and rustlers who, while working for the British, ranged over the neutral ground in New York, stealing cows from landowners and generally creating havoc through their raids.

However, close examination of older histories and early records raises the major question of whether these cowboys were Tories or actually American patriots.

For instance (with emphasis by italics added), James Smith, in his *History of Dutchess County,* published in 1882, wrote:

> During the [Revolutionary] war this locality [what is now the town of East Fishkill, N. Y.] was infested by bands of plunderers, employed by the British to obtain supplies, and known as "Cow-

boys." They usually carried on their depredations a short distance back from the [Hudson] river, and *paid but little attention to the political sentiment of those who owned such property* as they wanted or could sell, providing they could get it. The farmers throughout the county, when the cow-boys visited, feared them more than any other adversary, and thought as little of shooting them as they did a wild animal or an Indian.

In the year 1777, a party of the robbers came in this neighborhood and drove off several cattle and sheep, which aroused the farmers to a defense. One of the party strayed away from his companions and was caught by the infuriated yeomen and immediately hung without judge or jury. *In the performance of that execution several Tories were present and assisted, as they also had been victims of their lawlessness.*

And Benson Lossing, in his *Pictorial Field Book of the Revolution*, published in 1852, said:

The party called Cow-boys were mostly refugees belonging to the British side, and engaged in plundering the people near the lines of their cattle and driving them to New York. Their vocation suggested their name. *The Skinners generally professed attachment to the American cause, and lived chiefly within the patriot lines; but they were of easy virtue, and were really more detested by the Americans than their avowed enemies, the Cow-boys.*

In addition to which, in his *History of Dutchess County,* James Smith describes a relic preserved in the museum at Washington's headquarters in Newburgh, New York, as "a spontoon or half-spear used by Lieutenant VanWyck in hunting *Cow-boys and Skinners* in the Fishkill Mountains during the Revolution."

On top of that, John Paulding, David Williams, and Isaac VanWart—the three men who captured the British spy, Major John André, in 1780 in Westchester County—were identified at the time as "cow-boys."

All of which adds up to ample evidence that confusion did and does exist as to whether the cowboys of the Revolution were on the British or the American side. There is no confusion, however, as to their activities. They did raid the farms of the Hudson River valley and they did steal cattle.

The question is for what reason.

As for the early cowboys of Texas, there is confusion here, too.

"The next men [after the cowboys of Revolutionary days] who called themselves 'cowboys,'" Ramon Adams writes, "were a bunch of wild-riding, reckless Texans under the leadership of Ewen Cameron, who spent their time chasing longhorns and Mexicans soon after Texas became a republic."

And B. A. Botkin, in *A Treasury of Western Folklore,* has this to say about Cameron and his cowboys:

> Every district had its ranger company (in the days when Texas was a nation), commanded by some local veteran, whose members were ready to seize their rifles and sling on their powder-horns at a moment's notice. The young fellows from the Nueces were well known among the other bands for their iron endurance in the saddle, their faultless marksmanship, the boldness of their fighting.
>
> So it came [about] that they received a name from those with whom they rode pursuing Indians or Mexicans. And the term by which men called them stuck to them through the years. It fell to them quite naturally because of their vocation. They were known as the "Cowboys."
>
> It was the first time that the word was used west of the Mississippi, and always thereafter it retained its peculiar significance; it was handed down by these riders of the latter thirties to the booted herders who succeeded them, and so it spread all over the West.
>
> "Cameron's Cowboys" was the way that most men put it. For as his men stood out among the Texans, the leader whom they had chosen stood out among them—Ewen Cameron.

The period to which both writers refer is 1838–39, but other sources claim that this period was not that of the first Texas cowboys, and that Ewen Cameron was not the cowboys' only leader.

For instance, according to the historical documents of Mirabeau Buonaparte Lamar, who succeeded Sam Houston as president of the Texas Republic, the early cowboys of Texas were already an established band by that time, numbering more than a hundred. Lamar's papers, which do not explain where these cowboys came from, describe them as rustlers of longhorns who hated all things Mexican. In another reference to these cowboys, the Lamar papers state: ". . . Carnes commanded the Cow-boys [and] was the chief and leader of them." He was referring to a Scot named Neille Carnes.

And so, all that has been known up to now of the early cowboy in America is that he was a marauder during the American Revolution for either the British or the Americans—or both—and that he was already one of an established band in Texas long before 1829. It has also been known, of course, that both in Shakespeare's England and in seventeenth-century New England, a cow-boy was a boy on a farm who milked and tended cows.

A bit more of the puzzle is added in Owen White's *Texas: An Informal Biography,* with the statement, "[I]t is not surprising then that when a famous journalist, in 1940, visited Texas for the first time he was completely astounded at the spirit of its people. . . . He discovered, for example, that its founders had been men of the 'half hoss and half alligator' variety, who, having 'fit and drunk and cussed and died' only a short century ago, had left behind them a line of descendants who can still pass the bottle, and still cuss with an artistic vigor calculated to make even old Sam Houston himself very proud of them."

And author B. A. Botkin has also, on several occasions, pointed out that when a cowboy brags he often refers to himself as half horse and half alligator.

But no one has ever said why.

So the origin of the cowboy was a mystery made up of confusion, conflicts, and a puzzle.

Why should a man who spends his time in a saddle and his life on the plains call himself "half alligator"?

Why should Tory marauders capture their own side's highest ranking spy and turn him over to the enemy?

And, even more significantly, why should a hard-riding, straight-shooting, rugged, independent he-man who wrangles steers ever allow himself to be called a "cow-boy" in the first place?

Certainly all the conflicting identities of the cowboy cannot be wrong. Their sources are too reliable.

The truth lies in the fact that all are right—as far as they go. When they are all combined, a picture of the American cowboy as a man and the story of his origin and genesis begin to emerge. And he did have an origin, and he did have a genesis, and he deserves a place in American history.

The American cowboy did not just happen. His true origin, a full ten years before the American Revolution, was caused by his defense of an Indian, and served as a major springboard for the Revolutionary War itself. Only after gaining that freedom did he go west.

BY ERROR OR DESIGN

When, on July 15, 1691, two Dutch traders—Jan Sybrandt and Lambert Dorlandt—purchased a large tract of land along the east bank of the Hudson River from the Wappinger Indians, they had no thought of making history. Yet it was this simple act that set into motion a chain of events that eventually led to the creation of America's favorite hero—the cowboy. This is where and how it all began.

Contrary to later practices, in which the white man merely helped himself to whatever the Indians owned, the law in the British colony of New York clearly stated that, for a man to receive a grant of land from the Crown, he had first to purchase it from the Indians who owned it. This is what Sybrandt and Dorlandt did, and it was what others before them had done.

Although, at that time, anything north of the old Peter Stuyvesant farm (now the Bowery) was out in the country, and what is now known as Greenwich Village was more than two miles away from New York City, the land purchased by the two Dutch traders was a sensible investment. True, it was a good fifty miles upriver from the city, but there was, even then, settlement activity in that area, and there were good signs that such settlement would soon be on the increase.

The pre-Revolution cowboy of Dutchess County, New York

Dutchess County, in which the purchase was located, had been organized eight years earlier, and a few hardy settlers had already made their homes in the areas of Fishkill and Rhinebeck. In addition, adjacent land to the north of the Sybrandt-Dorlandt tract had been granted to another Dutchman, Francis Rombout, in 1685, while adjacent land to the south was in legal ownership of the Van Courtlands, and to the south of that of the wealthy and influential Frederick Philipse. So the entire eastern shoreline of the Hudson River north of New York City and reaching almost to Poughkeepsie was now in the hands of these few men.

For some reason Sybrandt and Dorlandt did not apply for a grant of the land they had purchased from the Wappingers, but simply held the Indian deed until 1697, when they sold their property to Adolph Philipse, son of Frederick. He immediately applied to New York's Governor Benjamin Fletcher for a grant of this tract.

What followed might have been the result of an error by Governor Fletcher or it could have been the result of collusion between the governor and Philipse, who was equally as influential as his father. If, however, it was an error, it was never called to Fletcher's attention by Philipse, and it was kept a secret by the entire Philipse family for almost sixty years. It was also the second contributing factor in the origin of the American cowboy. The deed that Sybrandt and Dorlandt had obtained from the Wappinger Indians covered land that lay between two points along the Hudson River—from a cliff known as Anthony's Nose to the mouth of the Matteawan Creek—and extended eastward into the woods a distance of three miles.

The deed conveyed to Adolph Philipse carried the same description. However, the grant covering this deed, which Adolph Philipse received from Governor Fletcher on June 17, 1697, extended eastward into the woods all the way to the Connecticut border, a distance of about twenty miles. Although the grant was illegal as the additional land had not been purchased first from the Indians, Philipse made no attempt to correct the error (if indeed it had been an error) and he never advised Sybrandt and Dorlandt or the Wappingers of the discrepancy.

In 1702, Frederick Philipse, Adolph's father, died and left his lands to a grandson, also named Frederick. In 1749, Adolph Philipse died, and left his lands to the same Frederick, who was his nephew.

In 1751, this Frederick died, and left both tracts of land to his three children—Philip, Susannah (Mrs. Beverly Robinson), and Mary. Mary and Susannah allowed Philip and Susannah's husband to more or less manage the holdings, particularly with regard to tenant farmers and their leases.

Philip Philipse and Beverly Robinson functioned well as a team. They were closer than many brothers-in-law, and most probably agreed between them to say nothing and do nothing about the additional land the family had acquired under the Governor Fletcher grant. It is a matter of record that they did not attempt to apply control over this questionable acreage until the year 1756.

The events leading up to that application of control began in the year 1740 within the tribe of Wappingers.

These Indians were peaceful and had always been so, even when they greeted Henry Hudson and his crew in 1609. Hudson's log tells how they came aboard the *Half Moon* day after day, bringing Indian wheat, beans, oysters, and tobacco in a "show of love," even after they had been attacked by some of the crew, who "durst not trust them."

Their culture was advanced. They were neat and clean, and their women were the fashion plates of their race and era. The men were tall, well-built, and proud of their heritage.

The Wappingers were a tribal division of the Mahicans, and their territory covered almost all of what is now Dutchess and Putnam counties. Each tribe had its own chief sachem, or king, who was responsible for the tribe's laws and treaties, and it was to this position, in 1740, that a young Christianized Indian rose. His name was Daniel Nimham. He ruled the Wappingers well, keeping them so peaceful that, through association with the settlers, many of the Indians spoke English, and many of the settlers spoke the Algonquin language of the Wappingers.

From 1740 to 1756, Nimham and his people continued to lease and sell small sections of their lands with nothing more than minor, normal problems from their tenants and buyers, and with no interference from the Philipse family.

Then, in 1756, the Wappingers were requested by Sir William Johnson, Superintendent of Indian Affairs for the colony of New York, to join with the British troops in the French and Indian Wars. Their reaction was far from enthusiastic until Philip Philipse and Beverly Robinson, knowing of, or having prompted, Johnson's request, convinced Nimham that fighting by the side of the British would be a wise move. It was also Philipse and Robinson who advised Nimham that, when he led his braves westward to battle, he should move all the old men, women, and children of the tribe to the mission at Stockbridge, Massachusetts, "for their safety." Thus did Philipse and Robinson rid the entire area of every single Wappinger.

For six years, Nimham and his men fought valiantly, and with great loss of life. They fell in southern Canada, in western Pennsylvania, and in eastern Ohio. A relative few, including Nimham, lived to rejoin their families at Stockbridge in 1762, and then return to New York. And their return was to give them no joy; it brought the shocking revelation that their lands were no longer in their possession.

All were gone—not only the tract running three miles inland from the Hudson River, which their forefathers had deeded to Sybrandt and Dorlandt, but everything east of it, all the way to the Connecticut border. Philipse and Robinson, in the total absence of the Indians, had applied the power of the illegal grant which had been given Adolph Philipse in 1697 by Governor Fletcher, and the discrepancy of which had been kept a family secret until this opportunity occurred—or was created.

There were but two strips of land in the area unaffected by the Philipse confiscation. One was known as the Oblong. This strip was about two miles wide and ran from the southern border of Massachusetts to Long Island Sound, parallel to the Hudson River, and lay as a buffer between the colonies of Connecticut and New York. Both colonies contested the other's claim to it, and it became a haven for the Quaker families who moved into the region seeking freedom of religion.

The second strip was a pie-shaped piece of land known as the Gore. It began at a point along the Hudson River between the Rombout and Philipse lands and fanned out to a width of about three miles, where it butted against the inland Beekman Patent. Both the Rombout heirs and the Philipses were contesting the other's claim to this strip, and it became a haven for independent settlers who preferred less tillable land to a lifetime of servitude as tenants of either land baron. It also became the area to which many of the Wappingers turned when they found their lands were gone. They had maintained a hunting village in the Gore for years, and knew the area well. In addition, as long as the ownership controversy continued, they were safe from both patroons.

It is a tedious task to tie together all of these apparently minor loose ends in setting the background for what subsequently took place, but each small fact has its own contribution to make in the birth of the

American cowboy. And when, for instance, it is pointed out, as it has just been pointed out, that an independent settler might prefer less tillable land to a lifetime of servitude as a tenant farmer, it becomes necessary to explain why.

A lease with a patroon was a far cry from a modern lease with a landlord. In the first place, many leases obligated not only the signer, but also his son, his grandson, and even his great grandson. Four-generation leases were not uncommon in the area. In addition, whatever personal property the tenant farmer moved onto his leased land became subject to immediate seizure by the patroon for even the slightest infraction of one of the many rules of the manor. And, even more importantly, a patroon had the power of life or death over each of his tenants and their families, and over any trespasser or suspected trespasser. This was the law of the land to which Nimham and his remaining tribesmen returned. These were the obstacles the Indian leader faced in any attempt he might make to recover his lands.

By error or design, the Wappingers were now a tribe without a home and, in his position as chief sachem, the responsibility for action belonged to Daniel Nimham.

SAMUEL MUNRO, WOODSRUNNER

Trying to recover his people's lands was a task that offered Daniel Nimham little hope of success. The Philipse family was powerful in the colony, not only because of their nationality but also because of their political associations and activities. They were part of the "in crowd"; the Indians, just as today, were not.

Nimham's task was additionally hampered by his choice of a possible peaceful solution over any show of force and, had he desired force, by his almost total lack of warriors due to their having been in the front lines during the French and Indian Wars, and consequently being the first killed. The situation seemed to be the result of careful and effective planning by the Philipses.

There was for the Wappinger chief but one course he could follow, and that was to journey to London and present his case before the British House of Lords.

This he did in 1762, taking a few of his tribe with him. And a more incongruous sight is hard to imagine than the powdered, white-wigged and black-robed members of the court sitting in formal session and staring, perhaps almost in disbelief, at these tall, muscular red men, their heads shaved except for a roach of stiff hair three inches high and three inches broad, running from their foreheads to the napes of their necks, and wearing moccasins and deerskin loincloths on bare bodies tattooed with the sign of their totem: the opossum.

The hearing was brief and resulted only in the Lords' promise to have the attorney general of the colony of New York "investigate the matter." The Indians returned to America and waited for the investigation to start and for a decision on their case.

They waited for the balance of the year 1762, and throughout the entire year of 1763. The formal claim for the return of their lands, which they had filed on July 28, 1762, went uninvestigated. The Philipse influence had kept it pigeonholed while that family continued leasing whatever it desired of the Wappinger lands to tenants of its own choosing.

Then, early in 1764, fate decreed that Daniel Nimham's path should cross that of an educated woodsrunner, or mountain man, named Samuel Munro. And it is interesting to conjecture what historic changes there might have been in the West had these two not met.

For one thing, the word cowboy might never have come into general and popular use. Secondly, ranch hands might have been recruited from a different source of manpower offering a less independent breed of worker. And, thirdly, Western movies, if any had been made, would probably have been known as *Steerman and Indian*, instead of *Cowboy and Indian,* films.

Little is known of the background of Samuel Munro, for the historians of the time, who wrote vanity books praising the landowners in order to sell more copies, brushed him off as a rabble-rouser and scoundrel. But from what can be pieced together Munro was the son of a Scot who had been arrested for failure to pay some bills and deported to the colony of Massachusetts as a slave to work off his debts.

In his search for freedom from such tyranny that imposed slavery on his father, Samuel left Massachusetts and settled in the one free spot he could find—a locale where land rent, at that time, was not collected, and where he could live without oppression. He settled in the area known as the Gore. It was here that he came to know the Wappinger Indians, and through continued contacts with them learned of Nimham's fate at the hands of the House of Lords, and the lack of action both by the attorney general and by the Governor's Council, where his formal claim had been filed.

That he was moved by what he heard is not surprising, based on his own background, and his desire to aid the Wappinger chief is easily understood.

By April of 1764, Nimham and Munro were close friends and allies. Wappinger council meetings had been called and Munro had addressed them, making well-conceived recommendations on how they could get action in the courts.

His plan was basically one of harassment of the Philipse family to a point where they themselves would insist that the Governor's Council hold a hearing on the legal ownership of the Indians' lands. The harassment was to be through persuading Philipse tenants to pay their rent to the Wappingers instead of to the Philipses.

Week after week Samuel Munro rode throughout the area, meeting with tenant farmers, convincing them of the validity of the Wappinger ownership of the land, and getting the tenants to agree to break their leases with the Philipses. Then, on November 6, 1764, he had the Wappingers appear before Dutchess County Judge Jacobus terBoss and Dutchess County Justice of the Peace John Aiken, and appoint him "their Attorney and Guardian of their Estates."

As such, he began dealing directly with Philip Philipse, Beverly Robinson, and a now second brother-in-law of Philip, Roger Morris. Except for causing all three to begin filing complaints on his involvement, Munro made little progress.

This was not enough for the dedicated Scot; he wanted immediate action. And so he began the second phase of his plan to harass the Philipses into bringing the claim to court. Munro began selling to each cooperative tenant the very land each was leasing, and gave legal deeds for each parcel sold. In addition, he published advertisements offering such deeds to all in the area who desired them.

This was too much for the patroons; the breaking point in their holdings was too close for them to ignore the situation; tenants were not only restless but were becoming rebellious. The Philipse family buckled under the pressure and, on February 6, 1765, just one year after the first meeting of Nimham and Munro, Philip Philipse, Beverly Robinson, and Roger Morris requested that the Governor's Council hold a "hearing on the claim made by Daniel Nimham, Jacobus Nimham, One Pound Poctone, Stephen Cowenham, and other Wappinger Indians to lands granted to Adolph Philipse *et al.*" The hearing was set for the following March 6.

Nimham's request for this hearing had been ignored for three years. The Philipses' request was granted and scheduled in thirty days. And this, in itself, should have been a forewarning of what was to come.

When notified, just two weeks before the date, that the hearing had been set, Munro and Nimham set out to find experienced legal counsel to represent them, only to find that the Philipse family had already hired every attorney in the colony—fifteen in all—to keep the Wappingers from having true legal representation. Through the political influence of the Philipses the hearing was a mockery of justice.

Held at Fort George in New York City, and presided over by Lieutenant Governor Cadwallader Colden and the Council (all of whom were "Gentlemen of Estates" and friends of the Philipses), the trial was to decide which of two documents was the legal one.

The first document was the deed sold to Adolph Philipse in 1697 by the two Dutch traders, Jan Sybrandt and Lambert Dorlandt. This deed carried the same land description as the one they had obtained from the Wappingers, and conveyed land along the Hudson River and extending eastward into the woods for a distance of but three miles.

The second document was the land grant to this parcel given Adolph Philipse that same year by Governor Fletcher. This grant erroneously described the conveyed land as extending eastward for about twenty miles, all the way to the Connecticut border. This was the grant already mentioned whose conveyance was kept a family secret by the Philipses until the Wappingers left the area to fight in the French and Indian Wars.

Well represented by legal counsel, the Philipse family presented its case, claiming that the entire parcel granted by Governor Fletcher rightfully belonged to them, charging the Wappingers with unlawful harassment, and accusing Munro of being the agitator of the Indians.

Having no true legal counsel, Nimham and Munro attempted to speak for themselves. The Indian chief was interrupted and cut short every time he rose, and Munro was threatened with jail if he so much as uttered one word. Then, when Nimham did manage to deny that the Philipse family had any right to lands other than those conveyed by the Sybrandt-Dorlandt deed, Beverly Robinson jumped to his feet and flashed a document that he claimed was a second deed from the Wappingers, given to the Philipses in 1702, and conveying the lands in dispute.

Nimham was refused permission to examine it, and when Munro picked it up from a table where it had been laid, a member of the Council snatched it from his hands and placed it out of sight. This deed, obviously, was what it was later proved to be—a forgery.

But, regardless of Nimham's claim that it was a forgery, and regardless of the fact that the law of the colony was that no such deed was legal unless it was recorded—and this deed, in sixty-three years, had never been recorded—the Council's decision was that the Wappingers had "no Claim to the Lands, and that they should give the Proprietors or their Tenants no farther Trouble, but suffer them to remain quiet and unmolested in the Possession of what so clearly appears to be their Property."

Although it was a clear-cut victory for the Philipses, it did not satisfy them. They accused Judge terBoss and Justice Aiken, who had handled the appointment of Munro as Nimham's guardian, of malpractice and ordered them to show cause why they should not be dismissed from office.

Even this was not enough. Every one of the eleven Philipse tenants who had offered, in vain, to testify for the Wappingers, was immediately dispossessed, all of their household goods were appropriated, and they and their families were left destitute. The Philipse family felt this was appropriate retribution. Then, in addition, the patroons had Munro arrested and jailed in Poughkeepsie for his part in siding with the Indians.

It was these acts, subsequent to the trial's outcome, that put Dutchess County in a state of rebellion and which were the final steps leading to the origin of the American cowboy.

The eleven ejected tenants, with the help of the Wappingers, were moved to the site of the Indian hunting village in the Gore on Stormville Mountain, where they became prime supporters of the now fermenting settler's revolt. Before Munro could get legal help to remove him from his imprisonment, a band of Dutchess men gathered and began a march to Poughkeepsie, with their ranks swelling as they marched until, when they reached their destination, there were 1,700 settlers who stormed the jail and released the Scot.

Now there was more than just the Wappinger cause at stake. Now the battle was brewing against all forms of manorial oppression. It was to be a battle that Munro and the dispossessed tenants, living in the Gore, would spearhead. And it was a battle that many settlers would join.

TURMOIL ON THE HUDSON

In 1765 almost the entire area from just north of New York City to just south of Poughkeepsie, and from the Hudson River to the Connecticut border, was still in the outright control of four families. The heirs of the Rombouts, the Beekmans, the Van Courtlands, and the Philipses ruled, in the strictest sense of the word, over a thousand square miles of territory. And located almost in the center of these combined manors was the Gore.

Still disputed as to ownership by both the Rombout family and the Philipse family, the Wappinger hunting camp located there was the natural headquarters for a rebellion. Samuel Munro and the dispossessed Philipse tenants, John vanTassell, Elijah Tompkins, Samuel Field, John Tompkins, David Paddock, Henry Fernander, Peter Angevine, Richard Curry, William Hill, James Dickenson, and James Philipse (no relation to the patroon) made it just that.

Log huts were built where longhouses had formerly stood. Families were made as comfortable as possible with equipment donated by other sympathetic tenants. And regular meetings of the men became more frequent, as their leader Munro formulated his plan to secure justice for the Wappingers and for all tenants of patroons. The Scot wanted strength, strength through physical numbers. The more tenants who could be recruited, the better his position would be in dealing with the lords of the manors, and the dispossessed tenants were his recruiting helpers.

Soon, others began joining his crusade. Stephen Wilcox, John Kane, Joseph Crane, Benjamin Weed, Isaiah Bennett, Moses Northrup, John Ferriss, Daniel Palmer, Jeremiah Fowler, and William Prendergast became members of Munro's levelers, as did many more from the Dutchess area.

By now, the Philipse family was becoming gravely concerned as well as furiously incensed. Through Beverly Robinson, additional involved tenants were evicted, leases were rewritten to give the Philipses more power over tenants suspected of becoming involved, and the militia was used frequently to instill fear into all tenants. And, where the militia was not used, other force and violence were.

Munro's answer to these acts was to extend his campaign for volunteer rebels into the holdings of all the patroons in southeastern New York. Notices were now posted across the lands, not only of the Philipses, but also of the Beekmans, the Van Courtlands, and the Rombouts. It was a call for all tenants to join Munro's crusade, and to pledge "That they would stand with lines and fortunes by each other; That they would suffer none of their party to be arrested for what they did as a group"; and "That none should agree with landlords until the whole did."

By word of mouth, meeting dates were set in different areas, and on these dates hundreds of farmers were to be seen marching in a body to the various meeting places. The ranks of the levelers grew to the thousands, with help being offered even from families in the adjacent colony of Connecticut.

Simultaneously with his recruiting activity, the Scotch leader kept the legal aspects of the Wappingers' case alive by having the tribe request permission for an appearance before the Privy Council in London for the purpose of appealing the decision of the Governor's Council. And to finance the trip for the Indians he had set up a lottery among the sympathetic tenants. The men of the Gore were missing no opportunities in what was now their battle for justice for all men, red and white.

Meanwhile, other forces from another source were being formed, and they, too, would play a major role in the birth of the American cowboy.

When, in 1765, the British Parliament passed the Stamp Act, which was the first direct tax levied on Americans, reaction in the colonies was far from enthusiastic. And in Massachusetts one group of men formed a secret organization with the purpose of finding ways to resist the tax. They initially called themselves "The Loyal Nine," but subsequently changed this name when they learned of an exchange of remarks that had occurred in Parliament during the debate on the bill.

One member had declared, "And now will these Americans, children planted by our care, nourished up by our indulgence until they are grown to a degree of strength and opulence, and protected by our arms, will they grudge their mite to relieve us from the heavy weight of that burden which we lie under?"

To which a Colonel Isaac Barré had answered, "They nourished by your indulgence? They grow by your neglect of them! As soon as you began to care about them, that care was exercised in sending persons to rule over them, in one department and another—sent to spy out their liberty, to misrepresent their actions, and to prey upon them; men whose behavior on many occasions has caused the blood of those sons of liberty to recoil within them."

The new name then chosen by the group was "Sons of Liberty."

Soon, Sons of Liberty organizations were being formed through the entire colony of Massachusetts, and throughout the colonies of Connecticut and New York, meeting with each other, and pledging mutual aid where needed. Their battle cry was "Liberty and Property," and their "Song for the Sons of Liberty" ended with the lyrics, "The birthright we hold shall never be sold,/But sacred maintained to our graves./And before we'll comply we'll gallantly die,/For we must not, we will not be slaves, brave boys,/For we must not, we will not be slaves."

Realizing that it would take more than the Stamp Act alone to arouse the public's ire against the Crown to the extent desired, the Sons of Liberty sought local examples of British injustice and publicized these in a series of printed handbills, leaflets, and booklets, which were widely distributed.

The fate of the Wappingers at the hands of the Philipses, the House of Lords in London, and the Governor's Council in New York was an excellent subject. Consequently one such leaflet was prepared by a member of the Sons of Liberty, Asa Spalding, who was also a Yale graduate and a lawyer in Norwalk, Connecticut. All of which established a contact between Munro and the Sons of Liberty, and led to an agreement of cooperative efforts against tyranny. And, to prove his sincerity, Spalding, as a practicing attorney, wrote to the New York Superintendent of Indian Affairs, Sir William Johnson, legally defending the Wappingers' lottery to finance their trip to England, which had come under violent attack by the Philipses and their attorneys.

As far as Munro was concerned the stage was now set as he wanted it. His recruiting of forces sympathetic to his cause had resulted in well over two thousand pledges of support. His band of resistors to manorial oppression was spread throughout the holdings of the major patroons, ready for his call to action. And he now had the additional support of the Sons of Liberty.

Action was not long in coming and, when it came, the men from the Gore did their job well. By early 1766, under the guidance of Samuel Munro, they had the area in a state of turmoil. Riots were frequent and great numbers of tenant farmers marched on the patroons shouting threats of vengeance.

It was commonplace to see a band of a thousand tenants heading toward one or another of the manor houses, and growing in size as it proceeded. The talk of the time was that, by year's end, every tenant in Dutchess and Westchester counties would join the cause of justice, and that this cause would be extended to include attacks of retribution on the governor and the Philipses' lawyers.

In an effort to control the farmers, British troops were kept jumping from one area to another. As fast as they would capture one leveler, a group of his fellow rebels would free him. The jail at Poughkeepsie was stormed weekly and prisoners freed to rejoin their cohorts.

By now, Munro's men were a veritable army, with "lieutenants" in charge of smaller groups. One of these was William Prendergast who, for a while, served as the leader's right-hand man. It was he who, with his avowed purpose "to restore the poor to their land," led many of the riotous marches against the Philipses and the Van Courtlands.

British troops tried again and again to capture Prendergast and Munro, but always without success, even though the governor had posted a sizable reward for their arrest.

Meanwhile, as the settlers' revolts continued in the colony, Nimham and six other Wappingers sailed for London to appeal again to a higher court for recovery of their stolen lands. But when they arrived they learned that the British Lords of Trade had been advised by New York's Governor Moore that the matter had been "thoroughly examined in the presence of a great concourse of people," and that their claim had been "found to be groundless." The governor also reported that great riots had taken place in Dutchess County, and that the Indians were at the bottom of these disturbances. He claimed that it was the Wappingers who were forcibly ejecting tenants from their homes on the Philipse lands, stating that such acts were instigated by their guardian, Munro, and labeling the Scot "as infamous a person as can be found in this Colony."

The Indians again returned home in defeat.

By this time, the settlers' revolt had grown into what New York history has chosen to call the Anti-Rent Rebellion, and the riots turned into blood-spilled battles between the 28th Regiment of the militia and the tenant farmers.

Bloodshed, however, had never been a part of Munro's plan, and the fact that some of his followers were dying for this crusade disturbed him deeply. And so the Scot called a series of meetings, which were held in the Gore in the late fall of 1766, and outlined his plan for a change of tactics.

Instead of confrontation, Munro proposed that his men stage a continuing series of raids on the manor estates and on the farms of those who sided with the lords of the manors. The goal of the raids would be to recover the confiscated possessions of the dispossessed tenants, or the equivalent of those possessions, with prime attention given to the recovery of livestock, especially the very necessary, and difficult to reacquire, cows.

Within a week the raids had begun. They were frequent and they were devastating. No patroon knew where Munro's men would strike next. The militia was of no use; not only could it not be everywhere at the same time, but when it did appear to guard one spot, an underground system advised Munro, and raids were averted to other locales.

Local histories of Dutchess County towns tell repeatedly of how "bands of men began to ride in the interest of dispossessed tenants," and how they would "raid the farms of pigs, chickens, horses, and cows."

As the raids continued, and the cow population of the manor farms greatly decreased, a new term of reference to Munro's rebels and levelers was born. This new name, given them by the patroons, and applied with all the hatred they could utter, was "cow-boy."

And so, in 1766, the American cowboy, or cow-boy, was born. It is interesting to note that the first cowboy was (like his present-day image) a rugged outdoorsman, dedicated to justice, and a rebel at heart.

He had become a cowboy because he had dared to stand up for the rights of an Indian chief to lands that had been stolen from his people. The fact that his action had developed into a Settlers' Revolt, and then into an Anti-Rent Rebellion, had never made him retreat from his original purpose of trying to acquire justice for the oppressed. The only difference was that, by now, his cause had been considerably broadened.

The cause was now so broad, in fact, that it was headed more and more, as days went by, by the Sons of Liberty. They successfully continued the raids of the "cow-boys," who by now had come to pride themselves on their new name, just as in the Revolution the American forces took pride in, and adopted, the derogatory tune of "Yankee Doodle," and they continued in vain to try to help the legal efforts of Nimham in reclaiming his tribal lands.

As the Revolutionary War approached, and the forces of rebellion grew and expanded their activities throughout the colony, numerous bands of opportunists began committing frequent acts of robbery and violence, and falsely identifying themselves as cowboys and members of the Sons of Liberty. By the early 1770's it was often difficult to tell who was truly a secret member of the Sons of Liberty and who was not. And the name "cowboy," by then, had become synonymous with the words "robber" and "bandit."

It was this broad application of the word that caused the confusion of identification during the Revolutionary War itself, when cowboys appeared to be working for both sides, and loyal only to themselves. As a matter of fact, the cowboys of the Revolution actually were composed of both the Anti-Rent Rebellion patriot cowboys and their professionally thieving namesakes who most often had Tory leanings.

But it was Munro's men, the men of the Gore, who in the Revolution continued their work with the Sons of Liberty; fought under Captain Abraham Swartout, Colonel Henry Ludington, and General Israel Putnam; and volunteered for espionage service with Captain Melanchthon Smith's Rangers.

These were the men who were America's first cowboys. It was these men and their descendants who subsequently carried their name and their characteristics westward.

WESTWARD WENT THE REBELS

By the end of the Revolution, Samuel Munro who, for almost twenty years, had been the dedicated crusader for the rights of the Wappinger Indians and freedom from feudalism for all men, and who had been the organizer and leader of America's first cowboys, was a tired and a disillusioned man.

The Wappingers had not recovered their lands and victory in the Revolutionary War did not bring an end to the manorial system of land ownership along the Hudson River. Ownership of large estates by a chosen few, with stringent, oppressive tenant leases, continued as in New York's colonial days. (It would, in fact, continue until adoption of corrective measures in the State Constitution of 1846, following a second anti-rent war which history calls the "Tinhorn Rebellion.")

In addition, age had begun to collect its toll from the Scotch rebel, and he chose to return to a quieter life in Massachusetts, with the satisfaction only of knowing that he had done his best.

As for the Wappinger chief, Daniel Nimham, he had given his life in the Revolution for the cause of the patriots in what could easily be interpreted as an act of retribution against the British, who had caused him and his people so much suffering. The story is best told in an account written in 1872 by Indian historian E. M. Ruttenber.

> The gallantry of the Oneidas and Tuscaroras during the [Revolutionary] war was only exceeded by that of the Mahicans and Wappingers. Active in the campaign of 1777, the latter joined Washington again in the spring of 1778, and were detached with the forces under Lafayette to check the depredations of the British army on its retreat from Philadelphia. At the engagement at Barren Hill they defeated a company of British troops, but not precisely in the manner of creditable warfare. Stationed in a wood at a considerable distance from the main army, they met the attack of the enemy by discharging their muskets and uttering their hideous battle-cry. "The result," says Sparks [an earlier historian], "was laughable; both parties ran off equally frightened at the unexpected and terrific appearance of their antagonists."
>
> But such was not their record in Westchester county (New York), where they first met the British, and where they were stationed soon after the engagement at Barren Hill. In July, while Simcoe and Tarleton [British officers] were making some examinations of the country, the Mahicans formed an ambuscade for their capture, and very nearly succeeded in their purpose, the party escaping by changing their route. Their most distinguished service, however, was performed in August. While on a scouting expedition on the thirtieth, Lieutenant Colonel Emerick met a body of them under Nimham, the king of the Wappingers, and in the engagement which followed was compelled to retreat (saving the lives of many patriot troops). On the following morning the whole of the British force at Kingsbridge was ordered out and the largest portion placed in an ambuscade, while Emerick was sent forward to decoy his assailants of the previous day. The plan failed, but an engagement was brought on, by Emerick's corps, on what is now known as Cortland's ridge, in the present town of Yonkers, which was one of the most severe of the war.
>
> The Indians made the attack from behind the fences, and in their first fire wounded five of their enemies, including Simcoe. Falling back among the rocks they defied for a time the efforts to dislodge them. Emerick offered them peace and protection if they would surrender; four of their number accepted the terms only to be hewn in pieces as soon as they reached his lines.
>
> The engagement was renewed; Emerick charged the ridge with cavalry in overwhelming force, but was stoutly resisted. As the cavalry rode them down, the Indians seized the legs of their foes

and dragged them from their saddles to join them in death. All hope of successful resistance gone, Nimham commanded his followers to fly, but for himself exclaimed, "I am an aged tree; I will die here."

And so, in 1778, near Tippets Brook in Westchester County, Daniel Nimham, chief of the Wappingers, gave his life in the cause of American freedom and independence. What few of his tribe were left chose Kent, Connecticut, and Stockbridge, Massachusetts, as their home. It was a sad end for a fine tribe of "loving people."

Now without a leader and still without the rights and privileges of land ownership, those cowboys of the Gore who had survived the war, their children who had grown in their image, and their still suppressed tenant neighbors, were also forced to look elsewhere for their personal freedom and independence. The lands to the west were the answer.

Years before Daniel Boone left his home in North Carolina to move to Kentucky and into the pages of American folklore, routes westward had already been established from Dutchess County to the Susquehanna River, to the Ohio River, and even to the lower reaches of the Mississippi River. Moravian missionaries from the Stockbridge area traveled some of these routes regularly in their efforts to Christianize red men. The Wappingers had also used some of these routes in their journey west to fight in the French and Indian Wars. And men from Connecticut, such as attorney Asa Spalding, who had spent much time defending Nimham, and others who were later to become leaders in the Sons of Liberty, had followed all of these trails in their effort to establish land company settlements on the Susquehanna, the Ohio, and the Mississippi.

Knowledge of the routes, of the beauty and fertility of the land they led to, and of the availability of this land was widespread among the men of Dutchess. And these were the routes that hundreds of the original cowboys, the sons and families of deceased cowboys, and their tenant neighbors followed as they turned their eyes and footsteps westward. The Aikens, the Shaws, the Tallmans, the Swartouts, the Prendergasts, and many others, all took that direction in their search for a true home.

It was not a mass exodus; it was not an organized migration. It was just that these men, in their demand for independence, preferred to go, as historian Frederick Turner described it, "to frontiers where a more liberal land policy prevailed." Other historians, those of the vanity type, expressed it differently, however: "Some of these landgrabbers transferred their activities to the Susquehanna, where Connecticut was presenting its claim to Pennsylvania."

True, some did settle in the Wyoming Valley of the Susquehanna River, where both states laid claim to title of the area until the dispute was settled by compromise in 1799. The majority, however, sought the shores of the Ohio and the Mississippi. These rivers became their new Hudson River, but they were Hudsons without the sailing vessels they had been familiar with.

These waterways south were waterways whose boats, in this period, were anything that would float: keelboats, barges, and flatboats, with the latter predominating. And, as the only accessible marketplace for what produce and livestock was to be sold lay downriver at New Orleans, the men from Dutchess County soon learned to handle these large rafts and thus became rivermen.

The flatboats were long, with a small cabin in the center. The decks were piled high with cargoes of flour, bacon, salt pork, and lard, or teamed with cattle and pigs. And the entire trip was by courtesy of the current of the river on its way to the sea. Two men, one forward, one aft, steered the raft to keep it on course.

In 1810, ornithologist Alexander Wilson provided this description of these rivermen: "As dirty as Hottentots; their dress a shirt and trowsers of canvass, black, greasy, and sometimes in tatters; the skin burnt wherever exposed to the sun; each with a budget, wrapt up in an old blanket; their beards, eighteen days old added to the singularity of their appearance which was altogether savage."

But, as savage as they must have appeared, they also are credited with having had a relaxed, but alert, quietness about them—the quietness of men who have found, for a while at least, a certain freedom they have sought.

During this period, and in this area, there is no historical reference to the word cowboy, as applied to these men from Dutchess. Another term takes its place, one that later was destined to become familiar on the Western plains in conjunction with cowboys. It came about because power from a river is available only in one direction: downstream.

When the Dutchess County rivermen reached their destination at New Orleans, they then faced the problem of getting back upriver. The water was flowing against them, so their flatboats were of no use. Consequently, when the produce and livestock were sold, so were their flatboats, which were broken up for lumber.

They then banded together for safety in groups of a dozen or more and took the only way home that was available, that of following the trails, such as the Natchez Trace, which led north. And, perhaps as much to keep their spirits up on the rough trek homeward, these half rivermen, half landmen, decided that, whereas on the trip downriver they had been "alligators," on the trail north they would be "horses."

Thus was born the self-appellation "half horse and half alligator," the descriptive phrase that later became a permanent part of the songs and the yells of the American cowboy.

ON TO TEXAS

According to one of its official publications, Texas is a state whose history "is a dramatic story of the great Southwest, of the mighty Western movement, of struggles to establish a free civilization. It reflects both the hardships and rugged pleasures of those who defied convention and nature while exploring and settling a raw new land.

"The environment of the land," the publication continues, "has been shaped not only by a frontier heritage, but also by the indelible influence of six different sovereign flags which have flown over Texas. A fusing of many different stocks of people has molded the unique destiny of the state."

Every word of this statement is doubtless true, but Texas, to a great majority of people around the world, connotes just one thing: cowboy. Regardless of the fact that the cowboy had his origin in Dutchess County, New York; regardless of the fact that the cowboy was a prominent figure in the Revolutionary War; and regardless of the fact that the cowboy subsequently spread himself over the entire Western area of the United States, the cowboy belongs to Texas. It was here that he was spawned,

The Texas cowboy of the 1820's

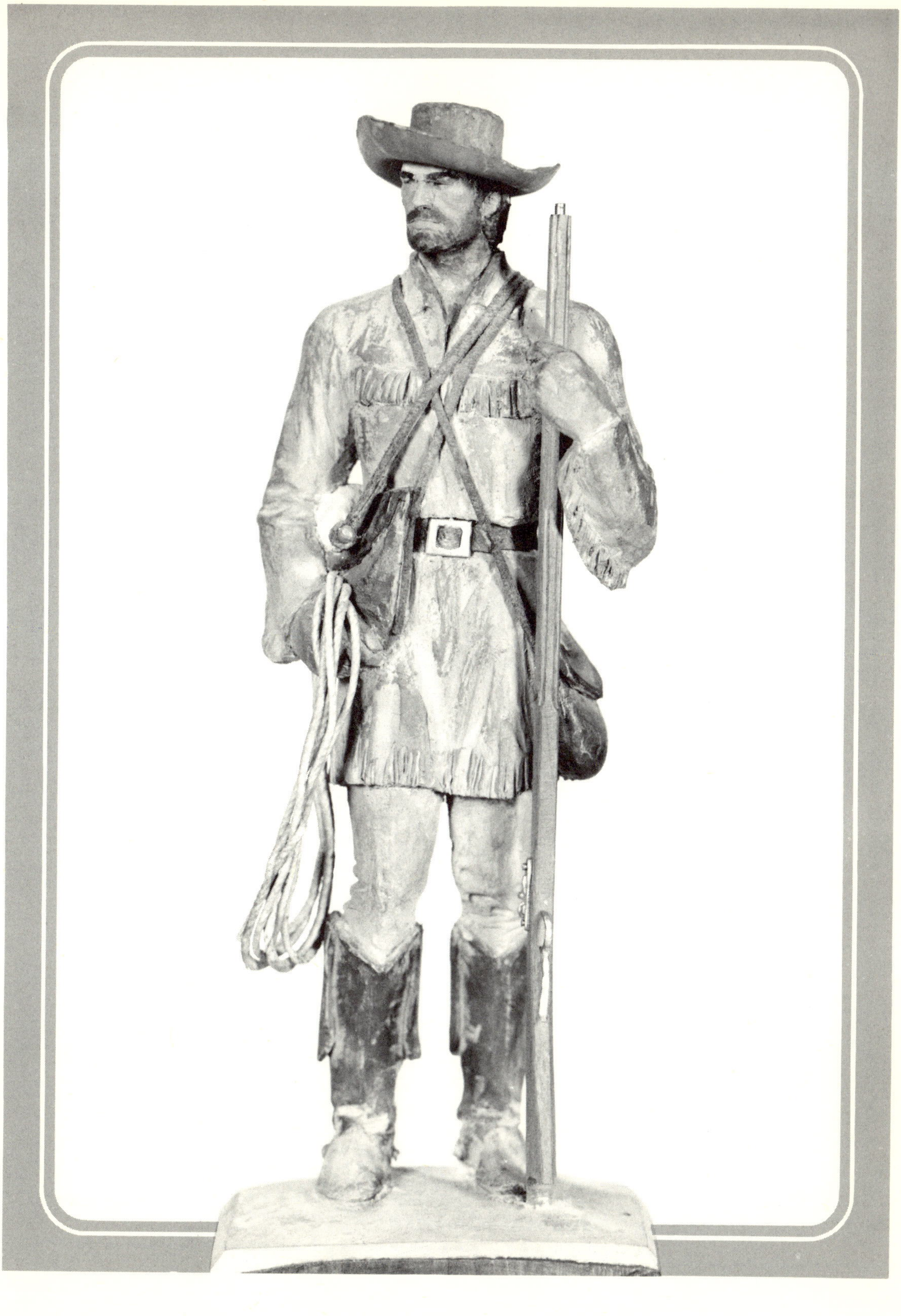

and it was here that he reasserted his demands for justice and independence—as he saw them. The cowboy and the state of Texas are inseparable, and well they should be, for the history of each is inseparable from the other.

Contrary to the belief of some, the first Texas cowboy was not an offshoot of the Mexican *vaquero*. The early documents of Mirabeau Buonaparte Lamar, mentioned earlier, leave no doubt that the first cowboys of Texas hated all things Mexican, and simultaneously proudly identified themselves as cowboys. To combine these two feelings in any human would be impossible.

Similarly, it does not hold that rugged men, handling longhorn steers, should feel that calling themselves cowboys was a cause for pride. Yet a logical explanation of this elusive point does exist. It not only explains the traditional pride in the use of the word cowboy, but also why cowboys, in their yells and songs, refer to themselves as half horse and half alligator.

For many of the men from Dutchess County, New York, the men who had been (or whose fathers had been) the Sons of Liberty cowboys of the Gore, now established along the Ohio and Mississippi Rivers, floating flatboats downriver and hiking home, it is hardly necessary to look further. But to learn when and why they came to Texas necessitates a brief look at Texas history.

Even before the year 1800, many American "land developers" had shown an interest in Texas, which at that time was a Spanish possession. And in 1803, just after the United States acquired Louisiana, one New Orleans writer reported that "Americans were spreading out [over Texas] like oil upon a cloth."

Then, in 1821, when Mexico won its independence from Spain and Texas became a state of the Mexican Republic, more than five thousand Americans moved in.

As Texas grew, so did the desire of its people for a government of their own, and it was inevitable that there would be a struggle for independence. The first clash took place on October 2, 1835, and one year later Sam Houston was inaugurated as the first president of the Republic of Texas.

It was during these years, between 1803 and 1836, that the cowboy introduced himself on the Texas scene, helping himself to the vast herds of longhorn cattle that roamed at will across the land between the Nueces and the Rio Grande rivers. Some of the herds were wild; others belonged to Mexicans. It made no difference to adventurous pioneers who viewed them only as a source of revenue.

As immense as the herds were, it was commonplace for several hundred head of cattle to be rounded up in a single night and started on a drive toward New Orleans markets. History admits that these raiders of longhorns were the first men in Texas to call themselves cowboys. They were already organized and operating as bands by the year 1829. Soon, these cowboys had even built pens along the trail to New Orleans for temporary corralling of the cattle and, in 1835, near Turtle Bayou, the first Texas ranch was established.

The cowboy had come to Texas to stay, and the key to his introduction into this state was in the person of Aaron Burr, statesman, lawyer, third Vice President of the United States and a man subsequently charged with, and acquitted of, high treason.

In 1804, with his political career ended as the result of his having killed Alexander Hamilton in a duel, Burr looked westward with plans that history has never been able to make clear. Speculations have ranged from forceful seizure of territory in Spanish America to the establishment of an independent republic in the American Southwest. Yet, neither in his diary nor in his voluminous correspondence is there reference to anything other than a legitimate interest in establishing a colonizing activity in the Southwest. In the words of his biographer, James Parton, "his schemes were genuine."

In July 1806 Burr purchased 400,000 acres of Texas land around the Washita River, a branch of the Red River. This was to be his base of operations. Here he could set up his own colony, far removed from the stigma that dogged him in the East. And, if war broke out with Spain, which seemed possible at that time, he could march on Mexico from there. His chief aide in this entire project was young Samuel Swartout, of the Dutchess County, New York, Swartouts.

One month later, Burr bade what he thought was his farewell to the East, and headed for the Ohio River, en route to Texas. Once on the river he halted everywhere, recruiting followers. With the help of Swartout, he had no trouble gaining former Dutchess County men as recruits from the Ohio area. Many joined him immediately; others promised to follow as soon as possible.

Meanwhile, unknown to Burr, a General James Wilkinson, another cohort of his in this operation, had been revealed as being in the pay of the Spanish. As a result, Burr's colonization movement came under suspicion. Then, in order to protect himself, Wilkinson turned on Burr and accused him of treason.

Unaware of Wilkinson's treachery, Burr, with his initial recruits and his flotilla, drifted down the Ohio and down the Mississippi, picking up additional supplies and more recruits along the way. It was not until he approached Natchez that he learned that he was being charged as a conspirator against his own country.

Immediately he surrendered to authorities with these words: "As to any projects which may have been formed between General Wilkinson and myself, heretofore, they are now completely frustrated by the perfidious conduct of Wilkinson; and the world must pronounce him a perfidious villain. If I am sacrificed, my portfolio will prove him to be such."

As for Burr's recruits—those who were with him and those who were following; the men whose roots lay in Dutchess County—they had no charges filed against them, and were allowed to continue on their journey to Texas. Many of them did just that, and Samuel Swartout, in 1807, wrote a letter to Sam Houston which included this excerpt: "By the way, eleven leagues of land is due me for my sufferings in that old Burr scrape. You need not say anything to the Mexicans, but I'm damned if I don't think they owe me a plantation for what I suffered in that expedition."

But it was Burr's recruits with their Dutchess County, Sons of Liberty, and flatboat roots, backgrounds, and traditions who had such a great influence on the state of Texas.

The early Lamar documents identify the first Texas cowboys as men from the Ohio River area, and many men from the Ohio were originally from Dutchess.

It is also interesting to note that, where the battle cry of the Sons of Liberty had been "Liberty and Property," the battle cry of the Texas Revolution was "Liberty and Texas," and the Texas men who fought in this revolution were also called "cowboys."

In addition, the traditional cowboy folksong "Red River Valley," which deals with the Red River in Texas, was originally titled "Bright Mohawk Valley," and dealt with the New York State area that served as the Dutchess County gateway to the West.

Suddenly, and for the first time in history, it becomes understandable why a rugged Texan who herded steers would be proud to call himself a "cow-boy," and why he would refer to himself as "half horse and half alligator," and why he would continue to cherish independence and demand justice. These were all a part of his personal heritage.

POINT 'EM NORTH

When, in 1835, the first Texas ranch was established near Turtle Bayou in Chambers County to take advantage of the longhorn drives to the New Orleans markets, its owner, James Taylor White, started traditional ranching in America. It was here in east Texas that modern ranching began.

Other men followed White to this area and also became ranchers, stocking their spreads with appropriated longhorns. And the men who rounded up these longhorns and sold them to the ranchers, and became ranch hands for these ranchers, called themselves "cowboys."

They did not call themselves "cattle hunters," as they would have done had they had their origin in Virginia or North Carolina. They did not call themselves "cowpen keepers," as they would have done had they had their origin in South Carolina, Georgia, or Kentucky. They did not call themselves "drovers," as they would have done had they had their origin in other Atlantic seaboard states. Nor did they call themselves *vaqueros,* even though the area in which they operated lay within the realm of Mexican influences.

These cattle handlers proudly called themselves "cowboys." And that section of Texas which ran from the northern Gulf Coast westward to San Antonio, then southwest to the Rio Grande River, and back to the Gulf, was their spawning ground. It was here that the Texas cowboy, still identifying himself as "half alligator and half horse" in his boisterous yells, became established as a ranch hand, using all the skills he had learned while helping himself to roaming longhorns.

After the year 1845, when Texas was admitted to statehood, even more ranches sprang up, and by 1860 there were more than three million head of ranch cattle in the state. Then, from 1861 to 1865, the Civil War brought with it the problem of what to do with these cattle, for Union blockades prevented the movement of any large herds which might have supplied beef to the Confederate Army. As a result, by the close of the war, Texas was overrun with cattle.

The supply was so great that longhorns were almost worthless, selling in the area for $3 to $4 a head. Yet at the same time, in the northern markets, butchers were paying $30 to $40 a head for the same animals. The problem was to get Texas beef to these northern markets, the only means being by way of railroads whose shipping points were almost a thousand miles away.

Nevertheless, in 1866, against almost insurmountable odds, the first command to "point 'em north" was given, and groups of Texas cowboys began the history-making drives of great herds of cattle toward the distant freight cars that rattled and rumbled across the northern plains on their way to St. Louis. Between the Texas ranches and the railroads lay not only seemingly endless miles, but also rivers that had to be crossed by forcing the cattle to swim them, Indians who might either politely ask for a steer or suddenly begin an attack, and armed Kansas farmers bent on turning the drives back out of fear of a cattle fever which longhorns could carry but to which they were impervious.

In spite of such hardships, over 250,000 head of cattle were pointed north that year in what could well be termed the birth of an empire, for the Texas cowboys' cattle drives have been called by many historians the greatest pastoral movement in recorded history. It was these drives which, over the years, were most responsible for opening up the West.

As these drives continued, a young Illinois beef dealer named Joseph McCoy became distressed at the number of cattle that were reaching St. Louis and the few that were reaching Chicago, and set out to do

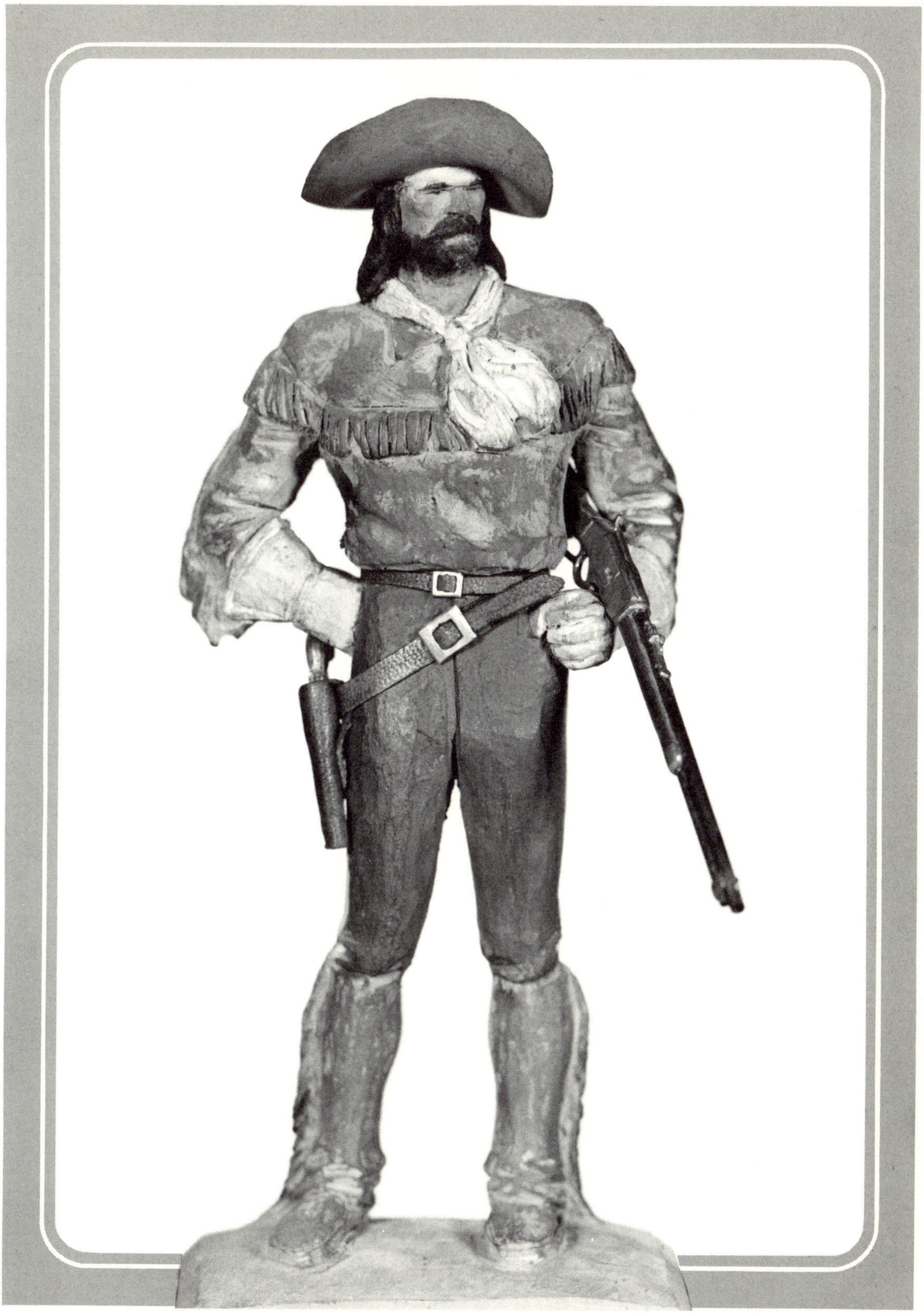

something about it. He made a deal with both the Kansas Pacific and the Hannibal and St. Joseph railroads to bring all the cattle he needed into Chicago, provided he could establish a suitable railhead in Kansas.

His search for this suitable railhead led McCoy to a small town with a population of about thirty people, none of whom objected to his plan, since they were so destitute they had nothing to lose by it. As small as the town was, however, it was nevertheless set in a large, grassy, well-watered area, and lent itself perfectly to McCoy's plans.

In July 1867 the Chicago beef dealer began to build a shipping yard, a cattle barn, an office, and a hotel. Railroad loading and switching facilities were installed and, within three months, the town of Abilene, Kansas, was set to become America's first true "cow-town."

Word of its existence was not long in getting around. McCoy saw to that personally by making numerous trips to Texas and spreading the news. As a result, Texas ranching began a migration and an expansion.

Where most Texas ranches had, to that point, been generally south and east of San Antonio, now ranchmen and cowboys began forging into areas of the state that would shorten the cattle drives, areas that previously had been not only undeveloped, but uninhabited.

As ranches were moved to or established in the Panhandle, across the extreme Western plains, and in the trans-Pecos region, their ownership took on an international big-business flavor. A British syndicate backed by Cunard Steamship Lines, a German tinsmith, a New York State judge, a Scottish earl, and a company whose chief stockholder was the prime minister of England, all became involved in Texas ranching.

And, as ranching grew into big business and the cattle drives increased in size and frequency, so too did the general interest in the men who were suffering the hardships and undergoing the dangers of bringing the herds to market. It was this interest, primarily among journalists of frontier towns, which led to the first general use of the word cowboy in its Texas meaning.

Where earlier newspaper reports had centered on the cattle, mentioning that a trail herd had arrived at a particular point, or that one had passed through a certain locale, the year 1870 saw the interest turning toward the human element of the drives: the cowboy. Accounts began to include descriptions of these men, calling them at first "cattle herders" and "trail riders." But, as the accounts continued and the journalists began interviewing these men, they learned that these riders already had their own name for their profession. It was then that the word "cowboy" began appearing in print in newspapers.

"The term 'cowboy,' when it did appear around 1870," according to the Texas Historical Association, "was always hyphenated and usually in quotation marks. Evidently the journalist felt he was coining a new word."

Fascinated with this new drama of the plains, curious editors in the East began sending their reporters westward to get firsthand accounts of this strange "newcomer" to the American scene. Story after story was filed, and column after column of newspaper space was filled with articles describing the cowboy.

One reporter, in 1873, wrote "The 'Cow-Boys' of Texas are a peculiar breed. They are distinct in their habits and characteristics from the remainder of even the Texas population as if they belonged to another race. The Lipan and Comanche are not more unlike the civilized white man than is the nomadic herdsman to the Texan who dwells in the city or cultivates the plains."

Another early reporter seemed, unknowingly, to be reflecting a description of the colonial New York forerunner of the Texas cowboy when he wrote "The 'Cow-Boy' is altogether the most free and independent fellow to be found in this peculiarly free and independent country."

These were the men who "pointed 'em north." They were, in the words of still another early reporter, "full of strange oaths ... boisterous ... but not hard-hearted." But unfortunately, over the ensuing years, paintings, literature, motion pictures, radio, television, Wild West shows, and rodeos have given the cowboy such a strong image as a romantic adventurer that his major contributions to American history have been ignored or forgotten.

In one form or another, the American cowboy, through his instigation of the Anti-Rent Rebellion of 1766, helped to bring about the American Revolution which gave birth to a nation and, through his pioneering of the great cattle drives north from Texas in 1866, helped to build an empire.

He should have earned a place in history as prominent as his place in folklore.

BROADER HORIZONS

Almost as soon as the first drive of Texas longhorns reached the freight cars in Kansas, ideas for an even greater expansion of the cattle industry were being formulated. Cowboys who were already feeling "crowded" in Texas and who had dreams of owning their own spreads, looked longingly toward the vast open ranges of Colorado, Wyoming, Montana, and the Dakotas. And settlers in those areas looked longingly at the obvious financial benefits to be gained from ranching.

The future was clear: Texas cattle would soon be on their way far beyond Abilene. So would cowboys, for where the longhorn went, there went the cowboy.

By 1870, the northern plains had become occupied, in the words of author Emerson Hough, "as if by magic, by the herds of enterprising ranchers who saw the rapid wealth that was to be accumulated under the constitution of the trade [ranching] in a new and favorable region [the northern plains]."

In 1866, the year that the first cattle were pointed north from Texas, a thousand head also left Texas for Montana. The adventurous, self-appointed cowboy who undertook this seemingly impossible drive of almost fifteen hundred miles through rugged and dangerous country was Nelson Story. Story, who was born in Ohio, left his home when he was eighteen and started west on foot with $36 in his pocket.

After a successful placer-mining operation for gold in Alder Gulch, Montana, he became aware of the lush grasses and fine brush shelters in the gulches where he had done his panning, and became convinced that this area could be a paradise for raising cattle. It did not take him long after that to recruit two helpers and leave for Texas.

Story purchased his longhorns in Forth Worth, hired some Texas cowboys, and started his drive back to what is now Livingston, Montana, where he established both modern ranching and the cowboy in that state.

Wyoming got its first permanent range herd and cowboys in 1868 when a man named B. B. Mills went to Kansas and bought 250 head of cattle, which were then driven back to Fort Laramie.

And, in 1869, when geologist and explorer John Wesley Powell was in the process of being the first white man to lead an exploratory expedition down Colorado's Green River, he found that two Texas cowboys were already grazing two thousand head of longhorns in the meadows along the riverbank.

In 1878, after the Black Hills area of what is now South Dakota was opened by law for settlement, a group of Texas cowboys and their longhorns were among the first to move in there.

By the year 1883, there were cowboys and cattle throughout the West. Then, in 1885, the great migration drives came to an end, for several contributing reasons.

Between 1866 and 1885, close to five million head of cattle had been exported from Texas, and many of the herds that had served to establish these new ranches had now multiplied into their own self-sufficiency.

Spur railroads had expanded into many previously untouched areas, and long drives to rail terminals were no longer necessary.

Texas tick fever had caused many areas to impose a quarantine on the importation of longhorns.

And many of the once broad and open trails leading north out of Texas were frequently blocked by barriers of barbed-wire-enclosed private holdings.

In 1890 the era of frontier America officially came to an end, so decreed by the U.S. Census Bureau.

So great had been the impact of the Texas cowboy on the frontier that, in just twenty-five years, from 1866 to 1890, he had converted it from what Daniel Webster had described as a "vast worthless area" to a major contributing factor in the development of the nation.

The cowboy had faced Webster's "region of savages and wild beasts, of shifting sands and whirlwinds of dust, of cactus and prairie dogs," had conquered it against all odds, and converted it to a financial empire. For this he has been rewarded only with such titles as "legendary figure" and "folk hero," and an occasional tribute in print.

Doane Robinson's *Encyclopedia of South Dakota,* for instance, says of the cowboy:

> The range cattle industry produced a unique population throughout the West, whose characteristics were emphasized by occupation and environment. Perhaps America has not anywhere developed a more efficient and self-reliant class than the cowboys—men who made the care of the wild cattle of the plains their vocation.
>
> They were a practical, hard-headed, courageous class, loyal to their employment, ready to make every sacrifice of comfort and to risk even life itself for the protection of their herds. While rather picturesque, their peculiarities have been grossly burlesqued. Tried by the natural law of the survival of the fittest, none but the most hardy could survive the rigors of this life.

And Emerson Hough, in *The Story of the Cowboy,* says:

> Certainly the man aspiring to the title of cowboy needed to have stern stuff in him. He must be equal to the level of the rude conditions of the life, or he was soon forced out of the society of the craft.
>
> In one way or another the ranks of the cowpunchers were filled. Yet the type remained singularly fixed. The young man from Iowa or New York or Virginia, who went on the range to learn the business, taught the hardy men who made his predecessors there very little of the ways of Iowa or New York or Virginia. It was he who experienced change.
>
> It was as though the model of the cowboy had been cast in bronze, in a heroic mold, to which all aspirants were compelled to conform in line and detail. The environment had produced its type. The cowboy had been born. America had gained another citizen, history another character. It was not for the type to change, but for others to conform to it.

Yet only a cryptic reference on New York State roadmaps marks the location of the birthplace of the cowboy on Stormville Mountain in Dutchess County. Only an obscure statue marks the area of their spawning grounds in southeastern Texas.

Little is known of the thousands of black cowboys who rode color-blind trails with their white counterparts, or of men like "80 John" Wallace, who was born of slave parents, became a working cowboy when he was fifteen, and went on to become the first successful black rancher in Texas.

History has shortchanged the American cowboy. Yet, although he has been declared on the verge of extinction many times, the American cowboy lives on. And many of his courageous characteristics, and sense-of-justice traditions—born of Samuel Munro on Stormville Mountain in New York's Dutchess County, and spawned by such men as Neille Carnes and Ewen Cameron in the heartland of southeast Texas—can still be found in modern cowboys on working ranches and in rodeo arenas.

The American cowboy has survived a Settlers' Revolt, an Anti-rent Rebellion, the American Revolution, the Civil War, and the encroachment of urban life. He has progressed from his birthplace in the Dutchess County Gore to Ohio, to Texas, across the Western states, and into the literature, art, folklore, and hearts of the nation, if not in its histories.

Of a particular breed that has not basically changed since 1766, he has become actor, writer, artist, businessman, politician, lawman, rancher, and rodeo performer, while always remaining a cowboy. Only a man with his rugged and courageous characteristics would have dared to face the challenge of thousand-mile cattle drives over unfamiliar country. And only a man with these same characteristics and a strong sense of justice would have dared to join Samuel Munro in his battle against the overwhelming power of the patroons of the Hudson River in defense of the rights of an Indian.

Fate has an intriguing way of shaping events, but it is interesting, nevertheless, to conjecture what the West might have been had not the hardy Texans "pointed 'em north," had there been no such men as Neille Carnes and Ewen Cameron, had Samuel Swartout not been a friend of Aaron Burr, had Aaron Burr been allowed to continue his journey to Texas instead of being accused of treason by General Wilkinson, had the Sons of Liberty not joined forces with Samuel Munro, had Governor Fletcher not voluntarily extended the Philipse land purchase beyond its limits and, most importantly, had Samuel Munro not chosen to aid Wappinger Chief Daniel Nimham. Would there ever have been a cowboy at all?

The truth is that all of these events did transpire and in a pattern that led to the establishment of the cowboy as the greatest of all American hero figures. Perhaps now, with the archeological artifacts from his encampment in the Gore preserved in New York's Brooklyn Children's Museum, and with this publication of his story, Samuel Munro will receive the honor that is due him for having been America's first cowboy.

Only in this way will future generations know why their favorite hard-riding, straight-shooting, rugged, independent heroes ever allowed themselves to be called "cowboys" in the first place.

PART
TWO

THOSE WHO FOLLOWED

A DEGREE OF RECOGNITION

The days of the frontier West are gone. Spur railroads and truck lines interlace the states that once were connected only by cattle trails. Ranches, to be successful, have been forced to become big business, and often corporate, operations, with ranchers spending most of their time studying new federal government programs, complicated changes in the tax structure, and market prices that fluctuate constantly.

The frontier cowboys are also gone and, except for the work of one organization, most would be on their way to oblivion. Fortunately, in the mid-1950's, a Kansas City garment manufacturer, Chester A. Reynolds, conceived a National Cowboy Hall of Fame where great Westerners could be honored in a national memorial. He then personally visited the governors of the seventeen Western states—Arizona, California, Colorado, Idaho, Kansas, Montana, Nebraska, Nevada, New Mexico, North Dakota, Oklahoma, Oregon, South Dakota, Texas, Utah, Washington, and Wyoming—and convinced them that they should appoint special trustees to found the shrine.

Ten years of diligent work by thousands of residents in the founding states followed. Then, on June 26, 1965, in Oklahoma City, Oklahoma, the National Cowboy Hall of Fame was formally opened.

Those who are honored here receive the honor as the result of nominations, which can be made by anyone who writes to the trustees of the particular home state of the nominee, giving the nominee's biography and listing reasons why that person should be considered. Such nominations are voted on by the trustees and, subsequently, by the executive committee.

Many cowboys and other great Westerners have been so honored. Many others have not yet had their names submitted. And still many more will never achieve this degree of recognition, because their identities have long since been lost to the memory of man.

Although it is usually referred to as the Cowboy Hall of Fame, this organization, literally, is the National Cowboy Hall of Fame and Western Heritage Center. As such, it is just as concerned with honoring great Westerners as it is with honoring great cowboys.

Great ranchers, whose financial investments in cattle helped to found a cattle empire but who were never working cowboys themselves, have been named to the Hall of Fame as honorees. So, too, have great explorers, great pioneers, and great politicians. All have, in some way or other, contributed to founding, developing, or strengthening the area of the West in which the cowboy lived and plied his trade, and so they deserve a place in the Western Heritage Center, even if not qualifying for the Cowboy Hall of Fame.

These honorees include such men as Jedediah Strong Smith, who was born near Binghamton, New York, in 1799, and at an early age moved with his family to Ohio, where he lived until 1822. In that year, at the age of twenty-three, he headed farther west to become an explorer and, from that time until his death in 1831, opened up many trails and territories that were later used by westward-bound pioneers. Honored also are men like Cyrus K. Holliday, who founded the Santa Fe railway system and, with a watch-charm compass and a ball of twine, laid out the city that became Topeka, Kansas, and Captain Richard King, who founded the vast King Ranch of Texas.

King was born in New York in 1824 and was apprenticed to a jeweler when a small boy. He shipped on a steamer bound for Mobile, and became a cabin boy at thirteen. Largely as a Gulf Coast river boatman, he became deck hand, pilot, and then captain. In 1847, during the Mexican War, he piloted the Rio Grande steamer for the United States, supporting the expedition of General Zachary Taylor. After the war, King formed a partnership with Captain Mifflin Kenedy for a steamship company on the Rio Grande. From 1850 until after the Civil War, the firm built or bought twenty-two steamers, and did an immense trade in cotton.

In 1852, riding horseback from Brownsville, Texas, to Corpus Christi, Captain King visualized a great future in land and, the following year, with profits from his steamship company operation, bought 15,500 acres of ranch land. He kept adding to this spread until, at the time of his death in 1885, his ranch holdings amounted to 600,000 acres.

Captain King was indeed a great rancher, Cyrus Holliday was indeed a great developer, Jedediah Smith was indeed a great explorer, and all were indeed great Westerners, worthy, along with their many counterparts, of being honored. But none was ever a working cowboy, and so, while deserving their places in the Western Heritage Center, they do not, for the purpose of this book, belong in the category covered by the Cowboy Hall of Fame.

It should also be noted that there is a great distinction between drovers and cowboys, and between buckaroos and cowboys, as well as between buckaroos and drovers.

Drovers were primarily farmers, or men employed by farmers, who moved sheep or cattle for relatively short distances to markets, or for long distances in family migrations. Those men, for instance, who drove the sheep and cattle across the country in the Mormon trek westward were drovers.

Buckaroo was originally a California term for a ranch hand, and the word comes from the Mexican *vaquero*, who was a herdsman of either sheep or cattle.

But, just as the original cowboy was a pre-Revolutionary War product of Dutchess County, New York, the Western cowboy is a product of Texas and, to be a true frontier cowboy, must have lineage or influences stemming directly from the Lone Star State.

It should also be recognized that, in order to qualify as a "frontier cowboy," that cowboy's major activity should have taken place prior to the year 1890 which, as has been stated, marked the official end of frontier America.

Close examination of the biographies of Cowboy Hall of Fame

honorees who could be classified as frontier cowboys, reveals that these fall into six categories. The first is that of cowboys who were trailblazers —those who opened up areas, who were the first to establish herds where herds had never grazed. Then there were frontier cowboys who became businessmen; frontier cowboys who became ranchers; frontier cowboys who became politicians; frontier cowboys who became lawmen; and frontier cowboys who became artists and writers, depicting in words or paintings a description of their own world.

Unfortunately, these honorees are only representative of thousands of other nameless frontier cowboys who, in their own way, contributed as much. Yet, in honoring these few, there is meant to be a degree of recognition for all.

The biographies that follow have been taken directly from information on file at the National Cowboy Hall of Fame. No attempt has been made to glamorize their achievements, as Cowboy Hall of Fame recognition is not based on glamour.

For many of these frontier cowboys, this marks the first time the story of their contributions and accomplishments has been told in print. This, hopefully, is some progress toward establishing the fact that the West was won, and that America was expanded, not necessarily by one particular style of revolver or rifle, but by the hard work and dedication of men known as cowboys.

COWBOY TRAILBLAZERS

After the New York followers of Aaron Burr had introduced the word cowboy to Texas in 1803, after Carnes' Cowboys and Cameron's Cowboys had made it something to be reckoned with during the 1820's, and after the first Texas ranch had established the term as a Texas way of life in 1835, it remained for others to spread the word across Texas and throughout the West. This they did immediately after the end of the Civil War.

They were men like Nelson Story, who drove the first Texas trail herd to Montana in 1866, whose life has already been described. And it was men like Story whose biographies follow.

JOHN SIMPSON CHISUM

As did the original Texas cowboys, John Chisum became a cowboy by helping himself to stray longhorns and building a herd. Then, early in 1867, he learned that the federal government was buying beef for the Navajo and Apache Indians and for the soldiers at Fort Sumner and Fort Stanton and other army posts.

Equipped with a power of attorney from other herd owners, Chisum left Denton, Texas, in June 1867, and headed for what is now Roswell, New Mexico. En route he picked up cattle bearing brands of those who had given him their power of attorney, and added them to his own collection of strays, selling them eventually to the government.

One of the first cowboys to "point 'em west," instead of north, Chisum continued to supply beef for soldiers and Indians in the amount of ten thousand head a year. In addition, knowing that grass was free for those who held the waterholes, Chisum gained control of these in the Roswell area, and soon staked out an empire that included a spread stretching from Roswell all the way to Pecos, Texas, with thirty thousand of his own cattle, hundreds of horses, and a hundred cowboys in his employ.

He was one of the West's great cowboy figures until the barbed wire fence and the plow destroyed the empire he had founded.

ROBERT SIMPSON FORD

A bullwhacker on the Santa Fe Trail when he was eighteen, a freighter on the Oregon Trail when he was nineteen, Robert Ford became a frontier cowboy trailblazer in 1870, when he was twenty-eight years old. He had been in charge of a sixteen-wagon merchandise train from Missouri to Sun River, Montana Territory. He took a liking to Sun River and remained there, first as a freighter, then as a cavalry haying contractor.

It was in 1870 that he saw the opportunities in raising cattle, and headed south for his own herd. He became the first to take cattle north of the Missouri River into northern Montana and into Canada. For the next two years he made numerous similar drives, acquired a Canadian contract to furnish beef for Canadian Indians and the Royal Mounties, and established ranches in Alberta, Canada, and Great Falls, Montana.

Ford was known not only as the father of the cattle industry in the Great Falls region but also as a "hip pocket" banker who was always ready to help another cowboy to establish his own spread.

CHARLES GOODNIGHT

In 1857 Charles Goodnight was a Texas Ranger and an Indian scout, which prepared him for his service during the Civil War as a scout and guide for frontier regiments. But as soon as the war ended, Goodnight became a cowboy, establishing his own herd in Palo Pinto County, Texas.

Seeking a better market than was offered in Texas during the Reconstruction period, he and a friend, Oliver Loving, decided to sell their herds in New Mexico. The route they chose to follow, in 1866, from Fort Belknap, Texas, to Fort Summer, New Mexico, became known as the Goodnight-Loving Trail, later one of the most widely used cattle trails in the Southwest. On their third trip westward over this trail, Loving was killed by Indians, but Goodnight got through, and continued to drive cattle to New Mexico for the next three years. In 1871, he and John Chisum combined their operations and cleared a profit of $17,000.

Goodnight laid out the Goodnight Trail in 1875, from Alamogordo Creek, New Mexico, to Granada, Colorado, and moved his herd there. But his Colorado ranching venture was not successful, and in 1876 he moved his 1,800 head of cattle from Colorado to Palo Duro Canyon in the Texas Panhandle.

The following year Goodnight entered into partnership with a rancher named John G. Adair, and built the J A Ranch into one that ran 100,000 head of cattle on a million acres of land. It was also Goodnight who developed an animal called a "cattalo" by breeding buffalo to Polled Angus cattle. The Texas Panhandle town of Goodnight is named for him.

CONRAD KOHRS

A native of Denmark, Conrad Kohrs emigrated to America in 1852 when he was seventeen years old, and later settled in Montana. First working as a miner, he switched to the life of a cowboy in 1874 and established one of the first breeding herds on the open plains of Montana.

Kohrs was a man who knew what he wanted, and felt best when he was doing the job himself. He rode the plains to get the cattle he needed, and trailed them to railheads in Wyoming and Utah for shipment.

By 1886 he had built vast ranch holdings, but the historic bitter winter of that year cost him 23,000 head of cattle, and almost totally wrecked him. With borrowed money, he bought more cattle and began again, building for himself a reputation as "king of Montana cattlemen."

OLIVER LOVING

Often referred to as "dean of the trail drivers," Oliver Loving became a cowboy in 1846 in Collin County, Texas. He was thirty-four at the time.

Three years later, he moved his herd to Palo Pinto County and, in 1858, was responsible for the first recorded movement of Texas cattle all the way to the terminal market of Chicago.

After the Civil War he became associated with Charles Goodnight in trailing cattle to New Mexico over their Goodnight-Loving Trail.

Loving also pioneered other trails: the one called the Shawnee Trail, which ran from Texas to Chicago, and a route to Denver, Colorado, which later became the Western Trail and was in full use twenty years after his first drive over it.

When he was dying, after the Indian attack, his last remark was reported to be "Don't leave me in foreign soil—take me back to Texas." Goodnight returned his body to Weatherford, Texas, for burial.

The towns of Loving, Texas, and Lovington, New Mexico, are named for him.

JOHN W. MYERS

John Myers became a cowboy in 1857 in Wyoming by trading one healthy work ox for two worn-out trail steers. He kept adding to these at every opportunity and, in 1862, registered the first brand in the state of Wyoming. In that same year Myers also created the first irrigation water right in the state, which has been in continuous use ever since.

His herd and his ranch in the Bear River Valley continued to grow and, at last report, the ranch was still being operated by his descendants.

DANIEL WAGGONER

In 1849, when he was twenty-one years old, Daniel Waggoner became a frontier cowboy in the wild and unsettled area of Wise County, Texas. His own stake was 242 head of cattle and six horses.

Locating near Decatur, he was soon able to afford the purchase of his own ranch and two hundred more cattle. Through wise trading and selling, his holdings grew until the Waggoner brand became the best known and most widely used in that cattle area, and until his cattle herds reached an estimated value of $7 million.

ELIAS W. WHITCOMB

An inveterate trader, Elias Whitcomb became a cowboy in 1866, as soon as longhorns were headed north by Texas cowboys. Leaving Colorado, where he had spent the winter of 1865, he headed for Texas, purchased his own herd, and drove it back to a homestead he acquired not far from where Cheyenne, Wyoming, is now located.

Whitcomb's cattle became the first permanent herd in southeastern Wyoming, and formed the basis for an extensive cattle-ranching operation.

And, even though he eventually moved into a mansion on Cheyenne's "Cattlemen's Row," he enjoyed proving he was still a cowboy, even with a gray beard, by riding horseback wherever he went.

FRONTIER COWBOY BUSINESSMEN

Just as there were frontier cowboys whose contribution to the development of the West lay in their pioneer trailblazing, so too were there frontier cowboys whose subsequent business careers contributed to the making of the West.

CHARLES F. COFFEE

After several ill-fated business ventures in his home state of Missouri, twenty-four-year-old Charles Coffee headed for Texas where, in 1871, he "hired on" as a cowboy, driving a herd of longhorns to Cheyenne, Wyoming, for the Snyder brothers. For two years he continued as a trail driver, before taking his savings and establishing his first ranch in Goshen Hole, Wyoming, in partnership with a brother-in-law.

When he was forty-one, Coffee, then living in Nebraska, and having had a series of successful ranching operations, turned his attention to banking and other business matters. By the time of his death, he owned outright, or had an interest in, eight banks; had become a major business developer of Chadron, Nebraska; and had "rendered valuable assistance" in the establishment of a state normal school.

But, never forgetting that he was a cowboy, Coffee was also greatly responsible for the building of the important livestock market in Omaha.

JAMES TAYLOR CRAIG

A native of Scotland, James Craig's first job in America was as a cowboy on a Wyoming ranch in 1885. Later he joined the John Clay organization and moved to Belle Fourche, South Dakota, where he rose from cowhand to superintendent of that company's Western Ranches, Ltd.

Subsequently he was elected vice-president, and then president of the John Clay Banks in the South Dakota communities of Nisland, Newell, Camp Crook, and Belle Fourche. He also served as a director of the Stock Growers' Bank in Cheyenne, Wyoming, and headed the campaign that built a new Butte County, South Dakota, Courthouse.

JAMES K. HITCH

Called a major developer of Oklahoma's Panhandle area, James Hitch became a cowboy at twenty-one when he joined a cattle drive to Kansas in 1876 and, with money borrowed from his boss, put two hundred head of his own cattle into the drive. The following year he participated in a second drive, this time with five hundred head of his own cattle. Hitch was on his way to success.

He settled in the Coldwater Creek area of Oklahoma, and helped to found the town of Guymon and Texas County. A good businessman and a leader in civic affairs, Hitch built the area's first school and first church.

TOM JONES

Tom Jones was a working cowboy who saved his money, and who broke horses for $1 a head to add to those savings. He moved to South Dakota in 1887, when he was nineteen, taking his own newly acquired small herd with him, and living in a dugout near Midland.

Continuing to work as a cowhand, as well as caring for his own herd, Jones increased his savings, and his holdings, until he was the possessor of 25,000 acres of range land.

As a businessman, he became a government appraiser, a partner in a livestock loan company, and founder of a bank, adding greatly to the development of the Midland, South Dakota, area.

MORELL CASE KEITH

Morell Keith was a cowboy in 1867, driving longhorns from Texas to Ogallala, Nebraska. That fall he started his own herd with a total of five head of cattle. Year after year he kept adding to his herd, and later formed a partnership with a friend, Guy Barton, of Omaha. By 1873, the value of the Keith-Barton herd was reported to be over $93,000.

In addition to his cattle activity, Keith engaged in construction work for the Union Pacific Railroad, operated a hotel in North Platte, Nebraska, and became a real-estate developer. He also was one of the original members of the board of directors of the Union Stockyards Bank of Omaha. Keith County, Nebraska, is named for him.

G. E. LEMMON

In the autumn of 1870, G. E. (Ed) Lemmon went to work for J. W. Iliff of Cheyenne, Wyoming, as a cowboy, trailing herds from Texas to Nebraska, Missouri, and the northern grass country.

In 1877 he joined the Flying V Ranch and, three years later, helped move its cattle to the Cheyenne River country of South Dakota. Later as foreman, and then as general manager of the Flying V, Lemmon is said to have saddle-handled more cattle than any other man of his time.

With his own savings, Lemmon acquired the lease on the Standing Rock Reservation which included 865,429 acres of land, and then used his time as a businessman to organize a stockmen's association. He founded and developed several towns in the state. He has been called "one of the prime architects and builders of the modern West."

FRONTIER COWBOY RANCHERS

In the frontier days of the West, there were some cowboys who, although choosing to spend their entire working life in the saddle, became either ranch owners or ranch managers. Eight men who fit into this category have been honored by the National Cowboy Hall of Fame.

SAMUEL BURK BURNETT

Samuel Burnett got his start in Denton County, Texas, as a cowboy driving cattle over the Chisholm Trail in 1869, after working for a year as a cowhand with the Wiley Robbins outfit.

In 1874, after many drives, he established his own herd carrying the 6666 brand, which became one of the state's most famous brands. After becoming a prosperous rancher, Burnett was the first man in the cattle business to buy a herd of steers to hold and fatten, which was the beginning of scientific ranching.

JAMES HENRY COOK

Having previously been a working cowboy in Kansas and Texas, James Cook began making trail drives from the latter state to northern points in 1876.

In that year he made one trail drive to Nebraska, and the following year drove a herd from southern Nevada to Idaho. Cook knew the West so well that he also served as a scout for the U.S. Cavalry and a guide for scientific exploration parties.

In 1882, however, he settled down in Socorro County, New Mexico, where he established and ran the W. S. Ranch. Then, five years later, he purchased the 0-4 Ranch on the Niobrara River in Sioux County, Nebraska. Here, he pioneered in importing purebred stock, helped organize stock growers' associations, and developed what became known as a model ranch.

MYRON D. JEFFERS

In the spring of 1869, Myron Jeffers decided to quit his job as an overland freighter and become a cowboy, even though he was thirty-six years old at the time. In that year he left his home in Montana and headed for Texas to buy a herd of longhorns and bring them back to sell.

This he did and, with his profits, made a second trip to Texas the following year for a larger herd, which he also brought back and sold.

Then, in 1871, he went to Texas for a third herd to bring back to the Madison Valley of Montana as foundation stock for his own ranch. A diary kept on this trip shows that the drive began on January 26 and ended on October 3, and that 1,894 head of cattle and thirty-seven horses were "road branded."

His Yellow Barn Ranch became widely known in the state, and Jeffers was recognized as one of Montana's most progressive citizens.

JOHN T. LYTLE

After the Civil War, twenty-one-year-old John Lytle returned to his home in Texas and took up the life of a cowboy on his uncle's ranch near San Antonio.

Later stepping out on his own, Lytle established a reputation as an excellent trail boss, operations director, and manager. Soon he was directing the movement of thousands of head of cattle on the trail, handling more than 450,000 longhorns, and delivering them in Kansas, Colorado, Montana, and other states and territories. During this period, he handled livestock with a total value of over $9 million—a record never reached up to that time.

In his ranching operations, Lytle had three partners: John W. Light, T. M. McDaniel, and Charles Shreiner. Their S—L and L—M brands were known throughout the Southwest.

THOMAS EDWARD MITCHELL

In 1879, Thomas Mitchell felt that the plains of southeastern Colorado, where large free-range outfits were operating, offered more opportunity and appeal than driving an ore wagon, and he decided to go there to become a cowboy.

Mitchell learned quickly and, in just a few years, his success was such that he was selected to be a trail cutter on the Oklahoma Strip.

It was during this assignment that he attracted the attention of the officers of the Dubuque Cattle Company, who represented banking interests in Iowa and had a large free-range outfit in northeastern New Mexico. They needed a manager and young Mitchell was persuaded to take the job.

He moved to the ranching headquarters in the Tequesquite Valley and remained a rancher the rest of his life. It was he who introduced the first registered Herefords into New Mexico, and founded the fine herd still carried there today.

JAMES PHILIP

An immigrant from Scotland at sixteen, James "Scotty" Philip immediately headed west, pausing in Kansas and then working as a freighter in Colorado and Wyoming before the discovery of gold in South Dakota's Black Hills in 1876 lured him there. The gold eluded him, but his new love for range land caused him to turn to the life of a cowboy.

As one who understood and got along well with the Indians in the area, Philip married a girl from the Cheyenne tribe in 1879 and settled down to ranching. Soon, using his own savings and some borrowed capital, he established the 73 Ranch near Fort Pierre, South Dakota, and became one of the state's largest and best-known ranch operators, with his brand recognized from the Black Hills to the Mexican border.

With unusual foresight, Philip feared the buffalo would eventually be killed off, and acquired five calves. He then converted his Fort Pierre ranch to a sixteen-thousand-acre pasture and brought his buffalo herd to nearly a thousand head. The Dakota zoo buffalo herds of today are the result of Philip's foresight.

BENJAMIN FRANKLIN WALLACE

Not what one could call a major rancher on his own, Frank Wallace nevertheless was one who was greatly responsible for the success of those for whom he worked.

Wallace was born to the life of a cowboy in 1860 on his father's ranch near Greenville, Texas, and had driven herds of cattle to Kansas over the Chisholm Trail by the time he was sixteen. He was a good cowboy and a dedicated cowboy; he even learned how to read and write from another cowboy. His entire life was built around ranching, and he knew this operation well.

It was Wallace who, in the positions of range foreman and manager, contributed so much to the successful operations of such outfits as the Hashknife Ranch, the NAN Cattle Company, and the Waters Cattle Company.

DANIEL CLAY WHEELER

Daniel Wheeler settled in 1861 in the Truckee Meadows of Nevada, where Reno now stands. He was but twenty years old, and had already spent four years of his life as a youthful gold prospector in California. But the life of a cowboy appealed to him and this was the area he chose for his work.

First as a cowhand, then as a small rancher, Wheeler built his herd and his holdings to a large cattle and land operation. He was among the first ranchers to import purebred sires into the region and to build up one of Nevada's outstanding breeding herds.

FRONTIER COWBOYS WHO BECAME POLITICIANS

Although it may be difficult to imagine a frontier cowboy becoming a politician, some did make that transition. These are those men who have been chosen by the National Cowboy Hall of Fame as worthy of recognition.

WILL C. BARNES

In 1883, near St. Joseph, Arizona, Will Barnes, former telegrapher-turned-cowboy, began buying sore-footed Texas cattle from westbound trail herds and set up his own small ranch.

By 1892 his spread included seven thousand cattle, and he had become a member of the Territorial Legislature. It was he who introduced and crusaded for the passage of a bill creating Navajo County, Arizona, which earned him the local title of "The Father" of that county.

A prolific writer, a fine pianist, and an accomplished storyteller, as well as a politician, Barnes is also referred to as one of the most versatile cowboys that Arizona ever produced.

CHARLES E. COLLINS

When he was sixteen years old, Charles Collins was already driving trail herds north and dreaming of someday owning his own herd. This dream came true, and Collins built up a spread that totaled 100,000 acres. His Colorado ranch had one of the largest commercial Hereford herds in the West.

Collins's involvement in political affairs, including his eventual election as a state senator, grew out of his assocation with the American National Cattlemen's Association, of which he was president four times, and his activity in federal credit organizations for the benefit of the livestock industry.

JAMES C. DAHLMAN

Born in Texas in 1856, James Dahlman left the Lone Star State when he was twenty after being involved in a gun duel, and trailed his way to Nebraska. There he found that, because of his rough appearance, no one wanted to hire him.

FRONTIER COWBOYS WHO BECAME LAWMEN

While it is hard to picture a frontier cowboy becoming a businessman or a politician, it is easy to imagine one becoming a lawman, and quite a few did just that.

In this category, there are six who have been honored by the National Cowboy Hall of Fame.

CHARLES FRANCIS COLCORD

In 1872, when he was thirteen years old, Charles Colcord was sent by his family from New Orleans to Texas for his health. He immediately became a cowboy, and learned his trade fast.

fifth grade, he set himself a course in self study during the years he was a working cowboy, which made him one of the best-informed and cultured men of his time.

After trailing a herd of longhorns to Lusk, Wyoming, Kendrick decided to remain in that state, where he later became roundup boss for the Wyoming Stock Growers' Association. From this position, he went on to become president of the association, a state senator, governor, and finally a U.S. senator.

JOHN SURVANT

A Montana cowboy, John Survant spent much of his life working for the Bloom Land and Cattle Company before starting out to establish his own holdings.

Success led him into politics, and he became a state senator. At age sixty, in a state election campaign, Survant proved he was still a cowboy by winning a rodeo calf-roping contest.

drove them north to a ranch he established on the North Platte River, near Fort Fetterman, Wyoming.

Irvine was a top cowboy and ranch manager and had always taken an interest in politics, becoming a member of Wyoming's Constitutional Convention, and a signer of the state constitution in 1890. He went on to become a state senator and state treasurer.

JOHN BENJAMIN KENDRICK

John Kendrick was orphaned early in his life and was raised by a half-sister and her husband. Although he attended school only to the

Finally, "Old Man Newman" took a chance on him, and Dahlman went to work on the Newman ranch north of the town of Gordon. And as the people in the area got to know him, they found they liked him, and later elected him mayor of Chadron for two terms.

Dahlman then moved to Omaha, but found he could not stay out of politics, and soon became mayor of that city, where, for term after term, the people of Omaha supported and re-elected their "cowboy mayor."

WILLIAM C. IRVINE

Billy Irvine settled in the sandhills of Nebraska in 1873 and worked as a cowboy on the Bosler brothers' ranch on Blue Creek. After three years with the Boslers, Irvine went to Texas, bought his own herd and

Three years later, when his father came for him, he preferred the life he was leading so much that he convinced his father to move the family to Texas and, with him, organized the Jug Cattle Company.

Setting off on his own, he moved to Arizona in 1884, and then to Oklahoma, where he became a chief of police under three different mayors, a sheriff, and then a U.S. deputy marshal.

JAMES WILLIAM FOLLIS

When Bill Follis was seven his family left their home in Texas and trailed their herd of cattle to Colorado, settling near Trinidad. Young as Follis was, he worked as a cowboy on the drive.

At the age of fifteen, now an experienced cowboy, he got the urge to strike out on his own, and moved to North Dakota, where he went to work for the Three Sevens outfit, rising to the position of foreman.

Known as a "cowboy's cowboy," Follis bought some land after the Three Sevens Ranch was sold, and established his own spread, while finding time to serve two terms as sheriff of Billings County. Hardly fitting the Hollywood stereotype of a Western lawman, Follis always insisted that there was relatively little gunplay in the West, and was irritated by allusions to "the wild and woolly West." He stated on numerous occasions that during both of his terms as sheriff, he could recall only one gun battle.

JOHN W. GOODALL

In 1876 John Goodall trailed a herd of cattle from Texas to Wyoming, and stayed on to work for an outfit in the Big Horn Basin. Later he moved to North Dakota to become foreman for the ranching operations of the Marquis de Mores.

It was Goodall who handled the first mass roundup in the Medora area, in which ten chuck wagons and a hundred riders participated, and in which Theodore Roosevelt, later President of the United States, acted as a tallyer.

Goodall later established his own ranch, and became sheriff of Dickinson, North Dakota.

BURTON C. (CAP) MOSSMAN

At the age of seventeen, Cap Mossman went to work as a cowboy for the Hat Ranch in New Mexico. By the time he was twenty-one he was foreman of an eight-thousand head ranch, and at twenty-seven he was manager of the Bloody Basin outfit in northern Arizona, gathering and trailing ten thousand steers through country in which use of even a pack pony was difficult.

At thirty he was general manager of the famed Hash Knife Ranch in Arizona, with a range of two million acres and sixty thousand head of cattle.

Mossman's exploits in running down rustlers in those days of the open range resulted in a request from cattlemen to get him to run the Arizona Rangers. Operating with but thirteen men, he succeeded in breaking up the rustler gangs.

GEORGE C. RUFFNER

George Ruffner settled in Arizona, near Prescott, in 1882, and immediately became a cowboy. Within four years he had acquired his own herd, registered his own brand, and learned intimately all the breaks and flats in the Agua Fria, Big Bug, and Chino districts.

Turning then to life as a lawman, he served first as a deputy sheriff and then as sheriff of Yavapai County. His hardest assignment, according to Ruffner, was the capture and hanging of a former cowboy friend convicted of murder, whom he trailed all over the Navajo country.

JOHN H. SLAUGHTER

John Slaughter grew up as a cowboy on a ranch near Lockhart, Texas, but left there after the Civil War, driving a herd of his own cattle to Arizona and settling on the San Pedro River, near the then new Tombstone silver discovery.

In 1883 he purchased forty thousand acres of the San Bernadino Mexican land grant, and it was at this Slaughter ranch that Geronimo surrendered to General Nelson Miles in 1886 after the Apache troubles in the area.

Slaughter had a reputation of being a brave and fearless man who could hold his own with all comers. Consequently, the many outlaws who infested Cochise County in the early Tombstone days generally gave his ranch a wide berth.

With the booming of Tombstone, however, more and more outlaws flocked into that section, and crimes of every description became common. For some reason, neither the efforts of Marshal Wyatt Earp nor those of Sheriff John Behan were able to control the situation.

Then, at the height of the troubles, John Slaughter was elected sheriff of Cochise County. It was he who rid that area of its outlaws, becoming one of Arizona's most noted sheriffs.

FRONTIER COWBOYS OF THE ARTS

With all of their stamina, their love of freedom, their dedication to adventure, and their adherence to the outdoors as a way of life, frontier cowboys were nonetheless human beings and, as such, it is only natural that some had talents in addition to those it took to be a cowboy.

Some of these men must have had singing voices that, today, would earn them roles in Broadway musicals, but it was not possible in those days to preserve a voice for future generations to hear. So these talents were lost with the loss of the man himself.

Other frontier cowboys had a talent for expressing themselves and describing their lives in the written word; others did the same with drawings. It is in these two areas that three men, honored by the National Cowboy Hall of Fame, stand out above other frontier cowboys. Because of their writing tablets and sketch pads the Old West has been preserved for history.

JOHN MARCELLUS (TEX) MOORE

Tex Moore was born to the life of a cowboy on a Texas ranch in 1865, near the present site of Fort Worth. In school he irritated his teacher with drawings of her in his McGuffey reader, drawings which emphasized her red hair and the wart on her nose. And in school, he constantly entertained his schoolmates with his "roguish jokes and humorous tales."

According to his biography, his life as a cowboy in Texas "covered a period in history that would be difficult to exaggerate as to the hardships which the early pioneers endured." Moore worked in the hazardous area between the Nueces and the Rio Grande rivers, and in the Texas Panhandle on the Charles Goodnight Ranch. Later he joined the John Chisum outfit.

While breaking a wild native Mustang he suddenly found himself on the ground, with the horse on top of him, rolling and trying to kill him. This made Moore lame for the rest of his life, and his painting of the incident started his career as a famous artist.

Giving up the active life of a cowboy, Moore began a career of both writing and painting. "His books," says his Cowboy Hall of Fame biography, "were written as the plain truth. His hand seemed to be made for the brush as he depicted the cowboy's life: the rambling of the cattle, the restlessness of the wild horses, and the natural grandeur of scenic wonders."

And the Texas legislature conferred on Moore the title "The Official Cowboy Artist of Texas" which even since his death has not been conferred on another artist.

EUGENE MANLOVE RHODES

From the time he was twelve years old, Gene Rhodes lived in New Mexico as a schoolboy, teacher, cowboy, and rancher. Always interested in literature, he seldom rode without a book in his saddle pocket.

Rhodes turned to writing because of his dislike for the inaccurate, distorted versions of Western life which others were writing. Dedicated to realism, he did not hesitate to use names of living persons in his stories; you could meet them in Santa Fe, Albuquerque, or El Paso. His books, written from personal experience, have always been accepted as factual.

His Cowboy Hall of Fame biography calls him "one of the West's outstanding authors; a man whose fiction had the accuracy of detail and description of undisputed fact as it related to terrain and livestock."

CHARLES RUSSELL

Charles Russell had two loves: the West and sketching. Even a term in a New Jersey military academy failed to change him. And so his father devised a scheme to cure young Charles of his desire to become a cowboy artist. He decided to send the sixteen-year-old Missouri lad to the Montana Territory to "get it out of his system."

In 1880, Russell landed in Helena and struck up a friendship with a hunter and trapper, Jake Hoover, who taught the boy much about the raw country he was in, its wild life, and its inhabitants.

Two years later, now eighteen, "Kid" Russell moved into Billings and went to work as a cowboy, trailing a thousand cattle into the Judith Basin. Then came jobs with other ranches, each bringing new experiences, and new subjects for his paintings.

When he was twenty-eight, he gave up the life of a cowboy to become a full-time artist. His Cowboy Hall of Fame biography calls him "The Cowboy Artist of the West," and says that he possessed "a thorough knowledge of all things early Western, a deep emotional feeling for them, and the genius to interpret them on canvas and in clay."

TRANSITIONAL FRONTIER COWBOYS

As the frontier West drew to an end and the term cowboy took on a new and glamorous popularity, there were certain cowboys who contributed greatly to this transition. Four of them have been elected into the National Cowboy Hall of Fame. All four were working cowboys who themselves became show business cowboys.

WILLIAM F. (BUFFALO BILL) CODY

William F. Cody is perhaps the best-known showman of his type the nation has ever known. He was born in Iowa in 1846 and moved to Kansas in 1857, where he immediately began working with freighting outfits. At fourteen he was a Pony Express rider, and at twenty-one acquired the nickname Buffalo Bill while hunting buffalo for meat for the Kansas Pacific Railroad construction crews.

    For four years, Cody was an army scout, and it was during this period that author Ned Buntline made him famous as the hero of his stories. Cody became a cowboy in 1877, after his army scouting days were over, first in Nebraska, and then in Wyoming. He later turned his attention to personal appearance tours in his Wild West Shows, which traveled all over the world.

TOM MIX

Tom Mix, in the words of his Cowboy Hall of Fame biography, was the one movie star "who had perhaps the greatest influence on popular fancy that developed the Western movie into its leadership of mass entertainment and helped perpetuate traditions of the range country."

Born in El Paso County, Texas, Mix, at age twelve, set up a one-gun shooting gallery with a gift .22 rifle to raise money to buy his own saddle, even though he had no horse of his own on which to use it.

He rambled throughout the West as a working cowboy, eventually joining the Miller brothers' 101 Ranch near Ponca City, Oklahoma. It was here that he started in show business, for the Miller brothers also had their own "101 Wild West Show," which Tom Mix soon joined.

After leaving the Miller brothers, he participated in Arizona and Wyoming rodeos, and then found his way to Hollywood, where he became one of the most popular cowboy actors of all time.

CHARLES HARLAND TOMPKINS

Charles Tompkins was born in Round Rock, Texas, in 1873. By the time he was fourteen he was a full-fledged working cowboy on the T-Diamond Ranch and had won his first steer-roping contest.

A veteran of four trail drives from Channing, Texas, to Miles City, Montana, handling five thousand head of cattle on each drive, Tompkins educated himself in bunkhouses and by campfires.

When the St. Louis Fair was being planned, he decided to try his hand at show business, and created a Wild West show for the exposition. One of his performers was a cowboy named Will Rogers. Tompkins never returned to the life of a working cowboy, but continued to produce and manage traveling Wild West shows which took the glamor of the old West to the four corners of the earth.

manage traveling Wild West shows which took the glamor of the old West to the four corners of the earth.

WILL ROGERS

Will Rogers, born in Indian Territory near Oolagah, Oklahoma, was a cowboy who became more than a performer. He earned the title of "humorist," "sage," and "philosopher," while gaining the respect and admiration of political leaders and nobility throughout the world.

From "Texas Jack's Wild West Show" to Broadway's *Ziegfeld Follies,* Will Rogers projected the image of a cowboy that had not been seen before and has not been seen since. It was he who was the personification of the cowboy as a human being and as a leveler, who had no use for pomp, no regard for title, and no fear of authority so long as truth and honesty were to be served. He could have ridden well with Samuel Munro, Neille Carnes, or Ewen Cameron.

RODEOS AND RODEO COWBOYS

In the days of the Old West, there were battles with rustlers, battles with Indian raiding parties, and personal shoot-outs—although not so many as novels, motion pictures, and television series would have the public believe—but the greatest battles the frontier cowboys fought were personal battles.

These were battles against the elements of nature, battles against the routine hardships of long trail drives, and battles against despair, and it took a certain breed of men to buck the odds against them in these battles time after time after time. Of such a breed were the frontier cowboys, and perhaps the closest to the hardiness of that breed among modern cowboys are the rodeo cowboys.

To quote *Top Op* magazine: "Put one of the best cowboys in the world on top of the meanest bronc in North America and you're in for eight seconds of unmatched drama and excitement. It's a display of strength, skill, courage, coordination, and determination that makes a man into a champion."

The appeal of becoming a rodeo cowboy is perhaps best summed up in the traditional rodeo statement, "There was never a cowboy who couldn't be throwed, never a bronc that couldn't be rode." The sport is looked upon as one created by men with competitive instincts born of a keen sense of manhood, and one which grew from spontaneous contests brought on by dares.

It is said that the first rodeo took place in Pecos, Texas, on July 4, 1884, when the foremen of several Texas ranches, familiar with the spontaneous contests of their cowhands, made these a part of the town's holiday celebration. Roping, racing, and riding contests were entered into by cowboys of the different ranches, with the ranch owners making up the purses for the winners.

Today, the rodeo has become a serious and highly competitive sport, attended by well over ten million spectators each year, and held in more than forty of the fifty states. One of the roughest, most entertaining, and popular rodeos is held each Sunday in October by inmates of the Texas State Penitentiary at Huntsville. And Colorado boasts of a saddle bronc riding school where experienced cowboys can become more experienced and neophytes can learn.

In 1936 the present Rodeo Cowboys' Association was organized (as the Cowboys' Turtle Association) although the need for some sort of organization was recognized long before that date. In essence it organized the sport by setting up rules and standards that would insure a "just amount of prize money," and provide honest judges and officials in all events. From that date on, the rodeo has had continuing success as an American sport.

Recognizing the contributions of rodeo cowboys to the lore, the reputation, and the appeal of the American cowboy, the National Cowboy Hall of Fame established a special category called the National Rodeo Hall of Fame. Only one honoree is elected each year by the board of trustees and, under present policy, only deceased rodeo cowboys are eligible.

The following rodeo cowboys are those who have been so honored. Their biographies are from information filed at the Cowboy Hall of Fame.

DOFF ABER

Doff Aber, world champion saddle bronc rider in 1941 and 1942, was born at Wolf, Wyoming, in Sheridan County, on a ranch to which his family had come years before in a covered wagon.

Aber grew up among cowboys. A handsome, slender young man, at nineteen he was entering professional saddle bronc riding competitions, and by 1935 had gained recognition as one of the best in the game.

Some evidence of his riding ability may be seen from the following: in 1935, the late Tex Austin produced a nine-day rodeo in Gilmore Stadium, Los Angeles. As a featured event, the top three contestants in saddle bronc riding were to make one final ride on each of the contest's six top horses. The leading trio turned out to be Aber, Pete Knight of Crossfield, Alberta, already a three-time world champion, and Earl Thode, then from Belvedere, South Dakota, and the 1929 and 1931 riding title holder.

The horses they rode were equally well known in rodeo circles: Five Minutes to Midnight, Ham What Am, Goodbye Dan, C. Y. Jones, Crying Jew, and Duster. Aber emerged the winner, riding five of the six. Only Ham What Am dusted the Wyoming cowboy.

A credit to rodeo, Aber, in his quiet, unassuming way, was an influential figure during the early days of the Cowboys' Turtle Association.

While recuperating from pulled leg muscles, Doff Aber was killed May 6, 1946, in a jeep wreck on his ranch north of Fort Collins, Colorado. He was thirty-six years old at the time of his death.

LEWIS EDWARD BOWMAN

Lewis Bowman was born at Brownwood, Texas, on November 27, 1886, and spent his boyhood on his grandfather's ranch at Weed, New Mexico.

Raised in the cattle industry, Ed Bowman followed the rodeo trail both as a roping contestant and a relay rider.

During an enforced layoff because of a broken leg, Bowman developed the first rope-working mount on the rodeo circuits. In order to help himself get hold of the roped calf in his crippled condition, he trained his horse to drag the calf back as he hobbled toward it. This maneuver proved so time-saving that Bowman kept the horse working in this manner when he returned to competition. Other ropers copied the new style and the modern "run-back" in roping horses was born.

Ed Bowman continued rodeo contesting until he was forty-four years old, and retired undefeated as the sport's greatest "strap and cinch" relay man, after competing nine years in the event. He died in 1961.

CLYDE BURK

Born in Comanche, Oklahoma, on June 14, 1913, Clyde Burk was national calf-roping champion four times—in 1936, 1938, 1942, and 1944.

A slender, wiry man who never weighed over 150 pounds in his life, Burk's quarter-Indian blood was evidenced in his high cheek bones, piercing hazel eyes, and black hair. It was said that no man was ever more contagiously likable or more sincerely admired by other men.

Burk's parents were tenant farmers, and he grew up knowing that he must carry his share of family responsibilities. When his mother died and his father three years later, the nineteen-year-old Clyde fought off outside pressures that insisted that his two younger brothers and two younger sisters be placed in an orphanage, and kept the family together himself.

His rise in the rodeo world came no easier yet, despite the handicap of his small size, Burk made himself into one of the greatest horsemen and ropers the sport has ever known. In this competition, where "the good big man is supposed to beat the good little man every time," he more than held his own.

Burk's death came at thirty-two, on January 21, 1945, at Denver's National Western Stock Show and Rodeo during the steer wrestling event. While he was hazing for New Mexico cowboy Bill Hancock, the steer ducked under his horse, causing it to somersault. The horse's full weight came down on Burk's head and chest, and he never regained consciousness.

CHESTER BYERS

In the words of fellow champions, "Chester Byers was the greatest trick and fancy roper of his era." And Will Rogers, himself a great roper, once wrote, "Chet knows more about roping than any man in the world."

Byers was such a bright star in the trick roping field, in fact, that many tended to forget he was also an excellent steer roper and a top-hand calf roper.

Born January 18, 1892, in Knoxville, Illinois, he moved with his family to Mulhall, Oklahoma, when he was three years old, and immediately decided to become a cowboy. Byers's first roping job was with the Pawnee Bill Show when he was but thirteen, and it gave him the roping fever. When he was fifteen, he went on tour with Lucille Mulhall's Congress of Rough Riders, and then continued to rope his way through old Mexico, Uruguay, Brazil, and England.

His first contest rodeo was in Los Angeles, California, in 1911; it was here he learned that he could make a living in rodeo competition. From then on, he regularly entered trick roping, steer roping, and calf roping contests all over the United States.

Although he made Fort Worth, Texas, his home, he was a featured trick roper at New York's Madison Square Garden for many years, and was World Champion in the trick roping event from 1916 through 1933, which was the last year in which a trick roping contest was held before his death in 1945.

LEE R. CALDWELL

Lee Roy Caldwell, in the memory of those who saw him in action, was "the greatest of all bronc riders."

Born in 1892 in Joseph, Oregon, Caldwell was the son of a rancher, and grew up helping to look after his family's cattle, which ranged on the Umatilla Indian Reservation. When he was sixteen he won his first bucking horse contest at Athena, Oregon, and began a career which, in the next decade, was to see him win every major riding title in North America.

Although there was no formal rodeo circuit as there is today, Caldwell, nevertheless, spent his entire time traveling throughout the United States to compete in the comparatively few rodeos which were held prior to World War I. In following this course, he became America's first professional saddle bronc rider.

By 1914 his name was a familiar one to all who knew bucking horses and riders and, by the time he was twenty-four, he had won prizes in numerous major rodeos and had been acclaimed Saddle Bronc Champion of the World.

A three-time winner in the Pendleton Roundup, Caldwell enlisted in the war against Germany, and captained a troop composed of Umatilla County cowboys who played a major role in the Saint-Mihiel offensive.

After World War I, he made his home in Stockton, California, where he died in 1952.

PAUL CARNEY

Among other titles he held, Paul Carney was World Champion Bareback Bronc Rider in 1937 and 1939, and All-Around Champion Cowboy in 1939.

Carney was born in Galeton, Colorado, on September 21, 1912, and began working with cattle and breaking colts almost as soon as he could walk.

He entered his first rodeo at Greeley, Colorado, when he was fifteen, and soon acquired the nickname Shanks. Verne Elliott, who produced the contest, took a liking to the eager, clean-cut youth, and offered him a job around the outfit to help him meet expenses.

The following summer, Carney won the Amateur Saddle Bronc Riding Championship at the Cheyenne Frontier Days Rodeo and, from that time on, made the rodeo his career. His first big rodeo triumph came in 1936, when he won the Bull Riding Championship at New York's Madison Square Garden Rodeo. The next year, also at New York, he won both the Saddle Bronc Riding Championship and the Bull Riding Championship, and was runner-up in the Bareback Bronc Riding event.

Carney was said to have been a natural leader among cowboys, and one who never tried to assert this leadership. His sense of humor was dry, but active, and he shunned practical jokes while delighting in good-natured ribbing. An all-around cowboy in the true sense of the term, Carney competed regularly and won consistently in steer wrestling, saddle bronc riding, bareback bronc riding, and bull riding.

In 1940, at the age of twenty-eight, he went into semi-retirement and invested in a dude ranch near Chandler, Arizona. He died of a heart attack in 1950.

BOB CROSBY

In every field of sports there are those who capture the public's fancy more than others. Bob Crosby of Roswell, New Mexico, was such a competitor in rodeo.

Born in Midland, Texas, on February 27, 1897, Crosby grew up as a working cowboy on a cattle ranch near Kenna, New Mexico. He turned to rodeo merely as a means of augmenting the family income.

The first big contest he entered was in 1923 at Yankee Stadium, New York City, and he walked off with $2,300 in prize money. Although a cowboy who participated in all rodeo events, Crosby never became a national champion in any one of them. He did, however, win the coveted Roosevelt Trophy for being the All-Around Cowboy Award winner for three separate years at Oregon's Pendleton Roundup.

His classic pioneer Western look, his Cross B brand, and his famous old black "lucky" hat, combined with the common knowledge that, during the latter part of his rodeo career, he competed with a leg which had never healed from its fifth fracture, added to his image and his popularity. *Life* magazine once called him "King of the Cowboys."

Crosby was killed in 1947 when a truck he was driving overturned.

EDWIN LOUIS CURTIS

Born near El Reno, Oklahoma, in 1908, Eddie Curtis was a grass-roots cowboy who made a name for himself from the very beginning of his rodeo career.

From 1928 to 1955 he competed in Saddle Bronc Riding, Bareback Bronc Riding, Bull Riding, and Steer Wrestling all over the United

States and in London, England, winning many All-Around Cowboy Championships.

One of the founders of the original cowboy rodeo organization, the Cowboys' Turtle Association, which later became the Rodeo Cowboys' Association, Curtis was active in both groups from 1936 to 1955. His genial personality, arena record, and business ability helped to improve relations between rodeo committees and cowboy contestants during the turbulent early days of organized rodeo. He died in 1965.

GEORGE (KID) FLETCHER

The National Bull Riding Champion in 1938, Kid Fletcher, or Fletch, as some of his fellow competitors called him, also once gained national publicity by being judged "the bow-leggedest cowboy in the world."

He was born in 1914 at Competition, Missouri, and raised in Hugo, Colorado, where he was introduced to the life of a cowboy.

Bitten by the rodeo bug when he was fifteen, he ran away from home to join Clyde Miller's touring Wild West Show. It was here that he learned the riding fundamentals which, in later years, made him one of rodeo's top competitors in bareback bronc riding, saddle bronc riding, steer wrestling, and bull riding events.

A man who had survived as many accidents in the rodeo arena as any other man in the sport, including multiple hip and arm fractures and a broken neck, Fletcher died in 1957 as the result of a head injury suffered while working on an electrical construction job.

PETE KNIGHT

Soon after his birth in Philadelphia, Pennsylvania, in 1903, Pete Knight moved with his parents to Alberta, Canada, where he broke two-year-old colts as a boy. At fifteen he entered his first bronc riding contest and came in second. In 1924, at the age of twenty-one, he lost the Prince of Wales Trophy by only .03 percentage points, but subsequently won it in 1927, 1930, and 1933 to retain permanent possession of it.

A world champion saddle bronc rider, Knight's championship record stood up for twenty years and, at the fortieth anniversary of the Calgary Stampede, he was named Number One of the four greatest competitors ever to compete there.

At Hayward, California, in 1937, Knight was thrown by a horse he had successful ridden five times previously and severely injured. Although he proved himself a true cowboy by walking out of the arena, he died on the way to the hospital.

WILLIAM E. LINDERMAN

One of rodeo's biggest money winners, and a six-time national champion cowboy, Bill Linderman was killed November 11, 1965, in a jet plane crash at Salt Lake City, Utah, while en route to meet with rodeo committeemen in the Pacific Northwest, in his role as secretary-treasurer of the Rodeo Cowboys' Association.

Linderman, who was born in 1920 at Bridger, Montana, drifted into the life of a cowboy on the Crow Indian Reservation, and soon was riding the "rough string." It was between horse-breaking jobs that he stopped off at a rodeo in Greeley, Colorado, and won $300 by riding saddle broncs. This launched his rodeo career.

In 1943 he won the first of his national rodeo championships, in saddle bronc riding—a feat he repeated in 1945. In 1950 he became the first cowboy to win three championships in a single season by winning the all-around cowboy title, the saddle bronc championship, and the steer wrestling crown. His second all-around cowboy championship came in 1953.

As much as anyone in rodeo, Linderman's life was dedicated to that sport. He served as an elected representative of the bareback bronc riding contingent on the Rodeo Cowboys' Association board of directors, and then became the association's president from 1951 through 1957, refusing the nomination in 1958. He is said to have had a fierce pride in doing well any job he tackled.

EDDIE McCARTY

Born in Loveland, Colorado, in 1887, Eddie McCarty was raised on a ranch near Chugwater, Wyoming, where he broke horses and worked cattle while he was growing up.

When he was twenty-three, he entered his first rodeo competition at Cheyenne's Frontier Days Rodeo, and won first place in the wild horse race. McCarty went on from there to become a top bronc rider, calf roper, and steer roper.

He was Steer Roping Champion twice at Frontier Days, and twice at the Pendleton Roundup, and was Bronc Riding Champion at Cheyenne in 1919.

One of the few men to ride the famous bucking horse Steamboat, McCarty was also part owner of two other famous bucking horses—Midnight, and Five Minutes To Midnight.

He died of a heart attack in 1946.

JAKE McCLURE

A rodeo contestant who has received the special recognition of being named an "At Large" honoree of the Cowboy Hall of Fame, rather than being named a Rodeo Hall of Fame honoree, Jake McClure was the winner of more prize money for roping than any other man in the sport up to the time of his death in 1940.

Born in 1903 near Amarillo, Texas, McClure grew up in Lovington, New Mexico, where he roped everything in sight on his father's ranch from the time he was nine years old. He began his rodeo career when he was fifteen, and subsequently roped calves in contests from New York to Texas and Oregon.

McClure was All-Around Champion Cowboy at the Pendleton Roundup in 1930, was awarded the Arizona State Championship Cowboy award in 1932, was the All-Around Champion at Phoenix, Arizona, in 1937, and won the Houston, Texas, Championship in 1939. He also captured honors in calf roping at New York's Madison Square Garden.

Will Rogers once said of McClure, "I know why Jake McClure wraps them calves up so fast. It's so he can hurry and sit down again."

COKE T. ROBERDS

Recognized primarily because of his pioneering in the breeding of quarter horses, Coke Roberds was nevertheless a cowboy in every sense of the word. He was an outstanding bronc rider, an exceptional roper, and one of the best heelers and forefooters in the livestock game. He could swim a herd of cattle across the Arkansas River when it was out of its banks, and did so many times.

Bearing one of the most famous names in quarter-horse circles, Roberds was breeding quarter horses long before the American Quarter Horse Association was formed. If a horse was Coke Roberds bred, or was out of one of his mares, it was registered without question. In fact, there is hardly a quarter-horse pedigree today which does not contain Coke Roberds' breeding.

Born in Texas in 1870, Roberds died in 1960.

LEE ROBINSON

Lee Robinson was born in Haskell County, Texas, on April 10, 1891, and worked on his father's ranch until he "graduated" into a working cowboy for other outfits.

The annual Fourth of July contests, which ranch hands held for fun, brought out his competitive ability and, in 1922, he went to Madison Square Garden where, against the toughest competition in the sport, he broke the existing record in calf roping. He was also a top steer wrestler, and won many individual championships in both events.

Robinson designed a low-cantle saddle tree which is still used extensively by ropers and bears the name "Lee Robinson Saddle." He was killed in an automobile accident in 1927 en route from the Tucson rodeo to the Fort Worth rodeo.

MARTIN T. (THAD) SOWDER

The first World's Champion Bronc Rider, Thad Sowder was born in Kentucky in 1874, moved westward to Iowa, and then to Colorado, settling on the Lazy D Ranch near Julesburg.

Sowder won his first bucking contest at Cheyenne in 1897, riding a horse named Five High to a finish, which, in those days, meant until the horse gave up. The title of World's Champion was first recognized at the Festival of Mountain and Plain at Denver, Colorado, in 1901. Sowder placed first, receiving the $500 Championship Rough Riders Belt and $150 in prize money.

He won the belt in Denver again in 1902, but there was a question raised about the victory, so Sowder agreed to a rematch the following day, which he also won, along with a side bet of $1,000.

He died in 1931.

HUGH STRICKLAND

Born in 1888 in Owyhee County, Idaho, Hugh Strickland ran wild horses with his father when he was a boy, and started competing in rodeos when he was in his teens.

From 1918 through 1926, Strickland won saddle bronc riding and single steer roping championships at such rodeos as those held at Pendleton and Cheyenne. He "bulldogged" for a few years, and was a good calf roper, trick roper, and trick rider.

He was married to Mabel Delong Strickland, acclaimed as one of the greatest rodeo cowgirls of all time, and was one of the first to advocate that rodeos should be "fast and snappy." It was also Strickland who, one year at Fort Worth, organized a group of rodeo cowboys into a polo team, and defeated an experienced army team from San Antonio in a three-game series.

Strickland, who died in 1941, is believed to have been the inventor of the bar-less, or hackamore, bit, but he failed to patent it and lost all claim to it.

WILLIAM LEONARD STROUD

Leonard Stroud was born at Monkstown, Texas, in 1893, and grew up in Clarksville and Honey Grove.

Practically unique in his versatility in the rodeo arena, Stroud was an acknowledged great trick rider, a World Champion Bronc Rider, and a competitor in trick roping, steer roping, and Roman racing. He also produced and directed his own rodeos.

His first big rodeo contest was at the Dallas Corn Exposition in 1914. Then, in 1916, at the Sheepshead Bay Rodeo in New York City, he won the championship in four contest events: bareback bronc riding, saddle bronc riding, trick roping, and trick riding. In 1918, he won the World Champion Saddle Bronc Riding title at Cheyenne.

Stroud delighted in planning and executing new tricks, such as roping four running horses while doing a head stand. He also originated many trick riding stunts.

Stroud, who died in 1961, was called "the greatest rodeo showman of his day."

FRITZ TRUAN

Born Frederick Gregg Truan at Ceile, California, on November 12, 1916, Fritz Truan grew up in Long Beach, far from a ranch, and actually taught himself to be a cowboy.

By the time he was nineteen, he was a full-time rodeo contestant, competing in bareback bronc riding, saddle bronc riding, and steer wrestling. By 1939 he was the cowboy the others had to beat.

He was World Champion Saddle Bronc Rider in 1939 and again in 1940. He was also the All-Around Champion of 1940. Four times during his rodeo career he successfully rode Hell's Angel, one of the great bucking horses of all time.

Truan enlisted in the U.S. Marine Corps in the fall of 1942. In 1945, during the assault on Iwo Jima, Leatherneck veterans of Guadalcanal, Tarawa, and Guam were crouched in a landing craft, grim and silent. The moment of mortal dread was at hand, when Sergeant Truan rose in defiance and roared, "Let 'er buck!" Iwo Jima was taken and became a symbol of victory.

After he was killed in action on February 28, 1945, the Marine Air Station at Kaneohe Bay, Hawaii, dedicated its rodeo field to Truan, who had starred there in an All-Serviceman's Rodeo in 1942. It was renamed the Fritz Truan Arena.

ORAL HARRIS ZUMWALT

Born at Morenci, Arizona, in 1903, Oral Zumwalt moved with his family to Roundup, Montana, where he entered his first rodeo contest, in the saddle bronc riding event, when he was thirteen.

Zumwalt continued as a contestant from that time on and won many events and championships, including calf roping at Billings, Montana, in 1930; saddle bronc riding, steer wrestling, and All-Around Cowboy at Nampa, Idaho, in 1933; and steer wrestling at Portland, Oregon, in 1935. In 1939, at Palm Springs, California, he bulldogged a steer in the record time of 2.2 seconds.

Zumwalt also set some sort of a rodeo record on a trip to Australia in 1937–38 with the United States Rodeo Teams. He not only brought back the All-Around Cowboy Championship, but also returned with the record for roping and tying a kangaroo.

A top pickup man, as well as a top contestant, Zumwalt was killed on June 10, 1962, while flanking a bucking horse at Montana's Big Timber Rodeo.

OTHER GREAT WESTERNERS

As for the great Westerners who have been honored by the National Cowboy Hall of Fame and Western Heritage Center—those who do not fit the category of frontier cowboys and have not been honored as rodeo performers—these should not be overlooked. Their contributions to the area that served the cowboy as home were too great to ignore.

Consequently, a capsule biography of each is presented here, listed under representative states, as a fitting conclusion to this book.

AT LARGE

Edward F. Beale (1822–1893)—trailblazer of an empire and developer of California's largest ranch

Warren L. Blizzard (1888–1954)—world-renowned Oklahoma animal husbandman

Frank S. Boice (1894–1956)—Arizona rancher and national cattle industry leader

John Edward Borein (1873–1945)—working California cowboy and Western artist

Christopher (Kit) Carson (1812–1867)—guide for Fremont and Kearny expeditions which helped overthrow Spanish control and open the West

Captain William Clark (1770–1838)—distinguished army officer who was co-leader of the Lewis and Clark Expedition

John Clay (1851–1934)—a native Scot who became one of America's leading ranch managers, and founder of businesses dealing with agriculture and livestock

Charles F. Curtiss (1863–1947)—famed dean of agriculture, and Iowa breeder of better livestock

Father Pierre-Jean DeSmet (1801–1863)—Jesuit missionary who spent his life among the Indians of the Northwest, to whom he was known as "Blackrobe," and outstanding mediator among the tribes and between Indians and the whites

General Grenville Mellen Dodge (1831–1916)—merchant, banker, Civil War officer, chief engineer in building of the Union Pacific and other railroads, and congressman

James J. Hill (1838–1916)—founder of Great Northern Railroad, colonizer, Minnesota empire-builder, land improver

Sam Houston (1793–1863)—soldier, statesman, first president of Texas Republic, governor of Tennessee and Texas

Captain Meriwether Lewis (1774–1809)—leader of famed Lewis and Clark Expedition, Virginia landowner, governor of Louisiana Territory

Henry Miller (1827–1916)—immigrant butcher boy who became a great California land developer and rancher on a giant scale

General William Jackson Palmer (1836–1909)—Civil War general, builder of the Denver and Rio Grande Railroad, Colorado industrialist and philanthropist

William MacLeod Raine (1871–1954)—dean of Western novelists, with eighty books, nineteen million copies

Frederic Remington (1861–1909)—painter and sculptor whose Western work shows true fidelity to subject and scene

Theodore Roosevelt (1858–1919)—North Dakota rancher, interpretive Western author, conservationist, President of the United States

Sacajawea (1787–1884)—talented Shoshone Indian woman who guided the Lewis and Clark Expedition from Dakota to the Pacific

Alexander H. Swan (1831–1905)—creator of great Wyoming ranches in intermountain area, importer of purebreds, builder of stockyards industry

Brigham Young (1801–1877)—Utah colonizer, state builder, Mormon exodus leader

ARIZONA

Ramon Ahumado (1868–1926)—superb horseman, roundup boss, and rancher

William Flake (1839–1932)—colonizer, stabilizer of northern region, area builder

Colonel Henry C. Hooker (1828–1907)—founder of oldest continuous ranch in the state, livestock breeder

Father Eusebio Francisco Kino (1645–1711)—Jesuit missionary, leader in development of agriculture and livestock raising

CALIFORNIA

William Hugh Baber (1893–1968)—one of the outstanding men in California's livestock and farming industry, civic leader, rancher

Fred Hathaway Bixby (1875–1952)—huge ranch operator, philanthropist, farm and livestock official

Henry C. Daulton (1829–1893)—overland trail maker, miner, rancher, public servant

W. C. (Wes) Eade (1874–1961)—rancher, cattle organization official, supporter of farm youth programs

Amadeo Peter Giannini (1870–1949)—founder and developer of the Bank of America, a builder of men, inspiring them with his tireless vitality and tempering them with his kindness

Colonel W. W. Hollister (1818–1886)—transcontinental drover, rancher, developer of vast areas

Collis Potter Huntington (1821–1900)—railroad builder, industrialist and financier, who helped build first transcontinental railroad

Dr. Charles Bruce Orvis (1858–1955)—pioneer veterinarian and stockman, improver of beef cattle

Richard Roy Owens (1881–1953)—stockman, noted contributor to better livestock

Joseph Russ (1825–1886)—pioneer livestock grower, business and political leader, philanthropist

Hubbard S. Russell, Sr. (1885–1963)—rancher, Western cattle producer, politician, and oil pioneer

COLORADO

William Bent (1810–1869)—frontiersman, Indian trader, fort builder

Charles Boettcher (1852–1948)—Prussian immigrant whose far-flung business interests included hardware, banking, beet-sugar factories, cement plants, electric light and power, meat packing, real estate, and ranching

John Evans (1814–1897)—a doctor who, after an outstanding career as a physician, church and educational leader in Indiana and Illinois, was appointed territorial governor of Colorado, becoming one of the greatest advocates of the state and the city of Denver

John W. Iliff (1831–1878)—cattle king, business leader, stockmen's official

Otto Mears (1840–1931)—Russian immigrant who was called "Pathfinder of the Western Slope" for building toll roads and railroads through mountains and plains

Nathan Meeker (1817–1879)—author, pioneer settler, Indian agent, philanthropist

Henry M. Porter (1840–1937)—outstanding industrialist banker, cattleman, civic leader and philanthropist, who contributed greatly to the building of Denver

John Wesley Powers (1838–1884)—early day wagon-train freighter who later became an outstanding cattle breeder, merchant, and legislator

Winfield S. Stratton (1848–1902)—gold prospector who struck it rich at Cripple Creek and used his millions to help develop his home town of Colorado Springs

Mahlon Daniel Thatcher (1839–1916)—a pioneer businessman, banker, and philanthropist, who contributed much to the state's development

IDAHO

Frank R. Gooding (1859–1929)—pioneer builder, governor, U.S. senator, stockman

John Haley (1835–1921)—Indian fighter, Oregon trail driver, cattleman, state builder

KANSAS

Dan C. Casement (1868–1953)—blue-ribbon breeder and feeder, stock association builder

Calvin W. Floyd (1872–1955)—cattleman, association official, banker, leading example of service

George Grant (1822–1878)—immigrant from Scotland who built a cattle empire, importer of first Angus bulls

Jesse Claire Harper (1883–1961)—veteran coach of many sports, succeeded Knute Rockne as athletic director at Notre Dame, prominent rancher and cattleman

Charles J. (Buffalo) Jones (1844–1919)—naturalist, who turned from slaying wild animals to preserving them

Dr. L. L. Jones (1879–1954)—veterinarian, cattle breeder, and rancher, who contributed much to the development of the Garden City area

Emil C. Kielhorn (1876–1946)—German immigrant who became a successful rancher, banker, and legislator, and who was diligent in the betterment of his community

Joseph P. McCoy (1837–1915)—builder of the stockyards at the railhead in Abilene, which gave birth to the development of the Chisholm Trail

William D. Poole (1829–1911)—developer and founder of one of America's oldest continuous ranches

MONTANA

Henry M. Holt (1848–1913)—rancher, livestock official, community builder

Adkin W. Kingsbury (1842–1924)—early pioneer, sheepherder, farmer, placer miner, and stockman

Mortimer Hewlett Lott (1827–1920)—miner and stockman who pioneered the settlement and development of southwest Montana

Charles Herbert McLeod (1859–1946)—early day merchant who played an important role in the state's political maturity and its community development

Peter Pauly (1871–1953)—one of the state's greatest cattle and sheep growers, later well known as an industrialist and a banker

Henry Sieben (1847–1937)—nationally recognized stockman, financier, and civic leader

Granville Stuart (1834–1918)—prospector who helped discover the gold fields of Montana, later outstanding as a cattleman, legislator, diplomat, and historian

William Wiseham Terrett (1847–1922)—livestock leader of southeastern Montana, developer of the JO Ranch

NEBRASKA

John Bratt (1842–1918)—territorial and state leader and developer

Edward Creighton (1820–1874)—builder of the first transcontinental telegraph line, rancher, developer of the plains country

George Ward Holdrege (1847–1926)—railroad builder and rancher, promoter of better agriculture in his area

Moses Pierce Kinkaid (1854–1922)—lawyer, jurist, congressman, whose "Kinkaid Act" allowed 640-acre homesteads

Frank J. North (1840–1885)—scout, first Sand Hills rancher, showman, stabilizer of wild country

William A. Paxton (1837–1907)—early railroad building contractor, legislator, business and civic leader

Bartlett Richards (1859–1911)—rancher, cattleman, banker, civic leader

NEVADA

Pedro Altube (1826–1904)—"father" of Basques in America, rancher and cattleman, Spanish Ranch founder

Lewis R. Bradley (1806–1879)—second governor of the state, builder and leader

Henry Hollowell Cazier (1885–1963)—civic-minded rancher and electric power developer whose enterprise contributed to the development of his state

William H. Moffat (1875–1963)—a native Californian who owned extensive ranching and packing interests in both Nevada and California, and is called the guiding spirit in the development of Nevada's livestock industry

John Sparks (1843–1908)—rancher on a vast scale, twice governor, states' rights fighter in Western expansion

William Morris Stewart (1827–1909)—attorney who helped form Territorial government and the state's constitution, counsel for great mining interests, served as Nevada's attorney general and six years as state's first U.S. senator, wrote the Fifteenth Amendment to the U.S. Constitution, and led the fight for remonetization of silver

NEW MEXICO

Holm Olaf Bursum (1867–1953)—well-known rancher who led statehood movement and was chairman of the Constitutional Convention

Victor Culberson (1863–1930)—cattleman whose skill built a vast spread, national stockmen's official

James Fielding Hinkle (1862–1951)—cattleman and banker who served his community and state as mayor, legislator, and governor

Solomon Luna (1858–1912)—large-scale cattle, horse, and sheep rancher, generous in community support

Lucien B. Maxwell (1818–1875)—first of the cattle barons from a small but adventurous beginning

Charles M. O'Donel (1860–1933)—manager of the great Bell Ranch for thirty-four years, one of the staunchest cattlemen in New Mexico's history, leader of both state and national cattlemen's associations

Charles Springer (1858–1933)—rancher, lawyer, pioneer road builder, principal writer of the New Mexico constitution

NORTH DAKOTA

J. M. (Murt) Buckley (1878–1962)—cowboy, horseman, and foreman of the great HT Ranch who later, as owner of his own ranch, contributed much to his community's development—famed for his fairness and good humor

William Connolly (1861–1946)—charitable rancher who encouraged better ranching and self-reliance, and whose faith and ingenuity "turned desert into paradise"

Matt Crowley (1875–1955)—ranchman and conservationist who left an indelible mark on his community

Alex Currie (1859–1937)—famed horse and cattle breeder, prophet of balanced agriculture

Frank Keogh (1877–1955)—well-known rancher who did much to organize and advance the welfare of his region

Daniel Manning (1845–1914)—horse breeder, rancher, pillar in area civic affairs and range industry

Wilse L. Richards (1862–1953)—leader in the cattle industry for sixty years; depression-burned in 1923, he "built again on the ashes"

Dr. Victor H. Stickney (1855–1927)—pioneer doctor, first and only physician for years in the western Dakotas, also left his mark as stockman, banker, and civic leader

Andrew Voigt (1867–1939)—pioneer rancher noted for his hospitality to Indians and whites alike

OKLAHOMA

Otto Barby (1865–1954)—conservationist and homesteader in "no man's land" who stayed when weaklings burned out

James A. Chapman (1881–1966)—oil pioneer of the Southwest

whose philanthropies have greatly advanced educational, charitable, and health institutions of the region

Thomas Gilcrease (1890–1962)—oil man, founder of Gilcrease Institute of American History and Art in Tulsa, farmer, rancher, real-estate dealer, banker, philanthropist

Ben Johnson (1896–1962)—ranch operator, champion roper, whose life linked historical events of the Old West and the new

Lynn Riggs (1899–1954)—author and playwright whose play *Green Grow the Lilacs* was the basis for the famous musical *Oklahoma!*, which has contributed much to Western American folklore

Sequoyah (George Gist) (1760–1844)—Cherokee Indian who, although completely unschooled, invented the syllabary that made his people literate

William M. Tilghman (1854–1924)—cattleman, frontier peace officer in Kansas and Oklahoma for fifty years

Reverend Samuel Austin Worcester (1798–1859)—missionary to the Cherokees in Georgia and Indian Territory, founded and made the Park Hill Mission an Indian cultural center

OREGON

Peter French (1849–1897)—pioneer cowman who started the purebred cattle business in southeastern Oregon, leader in the natural conflict between homesteaders and stockmen

William Kittredge (1876–1958)—builder of a cattle empire through ability and integrity, with interests including agriculture, reclamation, land and wildlife conservation, and improved breeding methods

Fred A. Phillips (1869–1964)—stockman, reclamationist, who helped draft the nation's farm credit program and headed it in his area for years

SOUTH DAKOTA

Ben C. Ash (1851–1946)—frontiersman, trailblazer, and peace officer

Tom Berry (1879–1951)—cattleman and legislator who, as governor, rescued the state from depression and drought

Al Clarkson (1866–1957)—horse breeder, cattleman, area developer and stabilizer, active in government and civic affairs

Newton Edmunds (1819–1908)—second governor of Dakota Territory whose policy of "negotiation not gunpowder" brought about favorable treaties with the Indians and closed the "War of the Outbreak," and whose utmost faith in Dakota in darkest days encouraged settlers to hang on

John D. Hale (1847–1929)—early-day ox-team freighter who later distinguished himself as a stockman

TEXAS

Stephen F. Austin (1793–1836)—colonizer, secretary of the Republic, state builder, and rancher

J. Frank Dobie (1888–1964)—widely known Western author and historian

Mifflin Kenedy (1818–1895)—rancher, cattleman, railroad builder, developer of South Texas

Edward C. Lasater (1860–1930)—rancher, dairyman, area developer, originator of a new hybrid breed of cattle

David D. Payne (1871–1969)—cowman, conservationist, and patriot who wholeheartedly subscribed to the principle of free enterprise

Captain Charles Armand Schreiner (1838–1927)—French immigrant who, starting from scratch, at one time owned more than a half million acres of Texas range land

UTAH

Joshua Reuben Clark, Jr. (1871–1961)—farmer, cattleman, lawyer, churchman, state and federal government official, served as Under Secretary of State and ambassador to Mexico

Jacob Hamblin (1819–1886)—colonizer, developer, pacifier of warring Indians, humanitarian

Anthony W. Ivins (1852–1931)—pioneer cattleman, peace officer, banker, church official

Jesse Knight (1845–1921)—developer of great ranches and other business enterprises, humanitarian

John A. Scorup (1872–1959)—cattleman, empire builder, public official

WASHINGTON

Arthur Armstrong Denny (1822–1899)—one of the founders of Seattle, pioneer business leader, legislator, congressman

Frank Miles Rothrock (1870–1957)—miner, purebred breeder, stockyards builder

Hiram F. (Okanogan) Smith (1829–1893)—pioneer settler, miner, cattleman, territorial official, developer

Benjamin E. Snipes (1835–1906)—cattle king, ruined in panic of 1893, he built again

Andrew J. Splawn (1843–1908)—a developer of the Northwest, first purebred cattle breeder, organizer of industry

Isaac Ingalls Stevens (1818–1862)—first governor of Washington Territory, instrumental in establishing territorial government and working out treaties with the Indians

WYOMING

Joseph M. Carey (1845–1924)—territorial and state official, U.S. senator, author of reclamation laws, rancher

Willis M. Spear (1862–1936)—rancher, cattleman, state senator, stockman, who was instrumental in bringing stability and order to the West

Francis E. Warren (1844–1929)—last territorial governor, first elected governor, U.S. senator, civic developer

BIBLIOGRAPHY

Abbott, Edward C. *We Pointed Them North.* New York: Farrar & Rinehart, Inc., 1939.
Adams, Andy. *The Log of a Cowboy.* Boston: Houghton Mifflin Company, 1927.
Adams, Raymond. *Western Words.* Norman, Oklahoma: University of Oklahoma, 1944.
Andrews, Israel Ward. *Washington County and the Early Settlement of Ohio.* Cincinnati: Peter G. Thompson, 1877.
Anonymous. *A Geographic, Historical Summary; or, Narrative of the Present Controversy, Between the Wappinger Tribe of Indians, and the Claimants Under the Original Patentee of a Large Tract of Land, in Philips's Upper Patent, So Called.* Hartford, Conn.: Green & Watson, 1768.
Bailey, Henry D. B. *Local Tales and Historical Sketches.* Fishkill Landing, N.Y.; John W. Spaight, 1874.
Bailey, Nathan J. *Johnsville in the Olden Time.* New York: Edward O. Jenkins' Sons, 1884.
Banta, Richard Elwell. *The Ohio.* New York: Rinehart & Company, 1949.
Barnum, H. L. *The Spy Unmasked.* New York: J. & J. Harper, 1828.
Becker, Carl L. *The Eve of the American Revolution.* New Haven, Conn.: Yale University Press, 1918.
Beirne, Francis P. *Shout Treason.* New York: Hastings House, 1959.
Benson, Egbert, *Vindication of the Captors of Major André.* New York: Kirk & Mercein, 1817.
Blake, W. J. *History of Putnam County.* New York: Baker and Scribner, 1849.
Boos, Staats, and Phillips. *History of East Fishkill.* Fishkill, N.Y.: Centennial Pamphlet, 1949.

Botkin, B. A. *A Treasury of American Folklore*. New York: Crown Publishers, 1944.

——, *A Treasury of Western Folklore*. New York: Crown Publishers, 1951.

Branch, Douglas. *The Cowboy and His Interpreter*. New York: D. Appleton and Company, 1926.

Bratt, John. *Trails of Yesterday*. Chicago: University Publishing Company, 1921.

Burr, Samuel Engle, Jr. *Colonel Aaron Burr*. New York: Exposition Press, 1961.

Carmer, Carl. *The Hudson*. New York: Rinehart & Company, 1939.

——, *The Susquehanna*. New York: Rinehart & Company, 1955.

Carter, Hodding. *The Lower Mississippi*. New York: Rinehart & Company, 1942.

Coleman, R. V. *Liberty and Property*. New York: Charles Scribner's Sons, 1951.

Cook, James H. *Fifty Years on the Old Frontier*. New Haven, Conn.: Yale University Press, 1923.

Daniels, Jonathan. *The Devil's Backbone*. New York: McGraw-Hill Book Company, 1962.

Dobie, J. Frank. *The Longhorns*. Boston: Little, Brown and Company, 1941.

Editors of *American Heritage Magazine. Cowboys and Cattle Country*. New York: American Heritage Publishing Co., 1961.

Frantz, Joe B., and Choate, Julian Ernest, Jr. *The American Cowboy: The Myth and the Reality*. Norman, Okla.: University of Oklahoma Press, 1955.

Grant, Bruce. *The Cowboy Encyclopedia*. Chicago: Rand McNally and Company, 1951.

Hart, Val. *The Story of American Roads*. New York: William Sloane Associates, 1950.

Hasbrouck, Frank. *History of Dutchess County*. Poughkeepsie, N.Y.: S. A. Matthieu, 1909.

Hatcher, Harlan. *The Western Reserve*. Indianapolis: Bobbs-Merrill Company, 1949.

Horan, James D., and Sann, Paul. *Pictorial History of the Wild West*. New York: Crown Publishers, 1954.

Hough, Emerson. *The Story of the Cowboy*. New York: D. Appleton and Company, 1897.

Huson, Hobart. *Refugio*. Woodsboro, Texas: The Rooke Foundation, 1953.

Ives, Burl. *The Burl Ives Song Book*. New York: Ballantine Books, 1953.

Johnson, P. Demarest. *Claudius: The Cowboy of Ramapo Valley*. Middletown, N.Y.: Scauson and Boyd, 1894.

Lomax, John A. *Cowboy Songs*. New York: Macmillan Company, 1936.

Lord, Walter. *A Time to Stand*. New York: Harper & Brothers, 1961.

Lossing, Benson J. *Pictorial Field Book of the Revolution*. New York: Harper & Brothers, 1850.

MacCracken, Henry Noble. *Old Dutchess Forever*. New York: Hastings House, 1956.

Mark, Irving. *Agrarian Conflicts in Colonial New York*. New York: Columbia University Press, 1940.

Martin, Joseph Plumb. *Private Yankee Doodle*. Boston: Little, Brown and Co., 1962.

Miller, John. *Origins of the American Revolution*. Boston: Little, Brown and Co., 1943.

Morris, Richard B. *Encyclopedia of American History.* New York: Harper & Brothers, 1953.

Nammack, Georgianna C. *Fraud, Politics, and the Dispossession of the Indians.* Norman, Okla.: University of Oklahoma Press, 1969.

Norton, Charles Ledyard, *Political Americanisms.* New York: Longmans, Green & Co., 1890.

O'Callaghan, E. B. *Documentary History of the State of New York.* Albany, N.Y.: Weed, Parsons Co., 1849 and 1850.

———, *Documents Relative to the Colonial History of the State of New York.* Albany, N.Y.: Weed, Parsons Co., 1853–58.

Parton, James. *Life and Times of Aaron Burr.* Boston: Fields, Osgood & Co., 1870.

Pelletreau, William. *History of Putnam County.* Philadelphia: W. W. Preston & Co., 1886.

Post, C. C. *Ten Years a Cowboy.* Chicago: Rhodes and McClure Publishing Company, 1895.

Robinson, Doane. *Encyclopedia of South Dakota.* Pierre, South Dakota: published by the author, 1925.

Roosevelt, Theodore. *The Winning of the West.* New York: Fawcett Publications, 1963.

Ruttenber, E. M. *Indian Tribes of Hudson's River.* Albany, N.Y.: J. Munsell, 1872.

Shumway, George; Durell, Edward, and Frey, Howard C. *Conestoga Wagon 1750–1850.* York, Pa.: Early American Industries Association & George Shumway, 1964.

Siringo, Charles A. *A Texas Cowboy.* New York: William Sloane Associates, 1950.

Smith, James H. *History of Dutchess County.* Syracuse, N.Y.: D. Mason & Co., 1882.

Smith, Philip H. *General History of Dutchess County.* Pawling, N.Y.: Published by the Author, 1877.

Thompson, Harold. *Body, Boots and Britches.* Philadelphia: J. B. Lippincott Co., 1939.

Turner, Frederick Jackson. *The Frontier in American History.* New York: Henry Holt and Company, 1921.

Van Doren, Carl. *Secret History of the American Revolution.* New York: Viking Press, 1941.

White, Owen P. *Texas: An Informal Biography.* New York: G. P. Putnam's Sons, 1945.

Wilson, Rev. Warren H. *Quaker Hill in the Eighteenth Century.* Pawling, N.Y.: Quaker Hill Conference Association, 1905.

THE ARCHIVES AND/OR REFERENCE DIVISION OF:

Adriance Memorial Library, Poughkeepsie, N.Y.
Arizona Library and Archives, Phoenix, Ariz.
California Department of Agriculture, Sacramento, Cal.
California State Library, Sacramento, Cal.
Connecticut Historical Society, Hartford, Conn.
Dutchess County Historical Society, Poughkeepsie, N.Y.
Kansas Livestock Association, Topeka, Kansas.
Kansas State Historical Society, Topeka, Kansas.
Kansas State Library, Topeka, Kansas.
Missouri State Historical Society, Columbia, Mo.
Montana Historical Society, Helena, Mont.
National Cowboy Hall of Fame, Oklahoma City, Okla.
Nebraska Public Library Commission, Lincoln, Neb.
Nevada State Library, Carson City, Nev.
New York Public Library, New York, N.Y.
New York State Education Department, Albany, N.Y.
New York State Historical Society, New York, N.Y.
New York State Library, Albany, N.Y.
Ohio State Library, Columbus, Ohio.
Oklahoma Department of Libraries, Oklahoma City, Okla.
Rodeo Cowboys' Association, Denver, Colo.
Sleepy Hollow Restorations, Tarrytown, N.Y.
South Dakota State Historical Society, Pierre, S.D.
South Dakota State Library, Pierre, S.D.
Texas Department of Public Safety, Austin, Texas.
Texas State Highway Department, Austin, Texas.
Texas State Historical Association, Austin, Texas.
Texas State Historical Survey Committee, Austin, Texas.
Texas State Library, Austin, Texas.
Wyoming State Archives and Historical Department, Cheyenne, Wyo.

(NOTE: Any material in Part I that is not specifically credited should be attributed to historical papers and documents in one or more of these archives.)

INDEX

Aber, Doff, *106*, 106–7
Abilene, Kan., as first cowtown, 44
Adair, John G., 61
Adams, Ramon, 10, 12
Ahumado, Ramon, 132
Aiken, John, 22, 24
Altube, Pedro, 136
American National Cattlemen's Association, 84
André, Maj. John, 11
Angevine, Peter, 25
Anti-Rent Rebellion, 29–30
Arizona Rangers, 92
Ash, Ben C., 140
Austin, Stephen F., 140
Austin, Tex, 106

Baber, William Hugh, 132
Barby, Otto, 138
Barnes, Will C., 82–83, *83*
Barton, Gruy, 72
Beale, Edward F., 130
Beekman family, 25, 26
Behan, John, 93
Bell Ranch, 137
Bennett, Isaiah, 26
Bent, William, 133
Berry, Tom, 140
Big Timber Rodeo, 129
Bixby, Fred Hathaway, 132
Blizzard, Warren L., 130
Bloody Basin Ranch, 92
Bloom Land and Cattle Co., 87
Boettcher, Charles, 133
Boice, Frank S., 131
Boone, Daniel, 33
Borein, John Edward, 131
Bosler Brothers ranch, 85
Botkin, B. A., 12, 13
Bowman, Lewis E., *107*, 107–8
Bradley, Lewis R., 136
Bratt, John, 136

Buckley, J. M. (Murt), 138
Buntline, Ned, 6–7, 8, 100
Burk, Clyde, 108–9, *109*
Burnett, Samuel Burk, 74–75, *75*
Burr, Aaron, 39, 40, 49, 57
Bursum, Holm Olaf, 137
Byers, Chester, 109–11, *110*

Caldwell, Lee R., *111*, 111–12
Calgary Stampede, 118
Cameron, Ewen, 6, 12, 49, 103
Canada, first cattle in, 60
Carey, Joseph M., 142
Carnes, Neille, 12, 49, 57, 103
Carney, Paul, 112–13, *113*
Carson, Christopher (Kit), 131
Casement, Dan C., 134
Cattle; drives, first, 42 ff.; industry, expansion of, 46 ff.; ranchers, in Hall of Fame, 57–66
Cazier, Henry Hollowell, 136–37
Chapman, James A., 138
Charles Goodnight Ranch, 95
Cheyenne Frontier Days Rodeo, 113
Chisholm Trail, 74, 80. *See also* Abilene, Kan.
Chisum, John Simpson, 58, 58–59, 60, 95
Choate, Julian, Jr., 3
Civil War, 42
Clark, Joshua Reuben, Jr., 141
Clark, Capt., William, 131
Clarkson, Al, 140
Clay, John, 69, 131

Clyde Miller's Wild West Show, 117
Cody, William F. (Buffalo Bill), 7, 99–100, *100*
Coffee, Charles F., 67–68, *68*
Colcord, Charles Francis, 88–89, *89*
Colden, Cadwallader, 23
Collins, Charles E., 83–84, *84*
Connolly, William, 138
Cook, James H., 75–76, *76*
Cooper, Gary, 8
Cowboy(s): artists, 94–98; black, 48; businessmen, 67–73; definitions of, 3–8; description, 45; lawmen, 88–93; name, origin of, 13, 29, 30, 34, 35, 38, 40, 41–42, 44–45; origin of, 9–13, 14–19; politicians, 82–87; ranchowners, 74–81; rodeo, 105–29; showbusiness, 99–103; trailblazers, 57–66
Cowboys' Turtle Association, 105, 107, 116
Cowenham, Stephen, 22
Craig, James T., *69*, 69
Crane, Joseph, 26
Creighton, Edward, 136
Crosby, Bob, *114*, 114–15
Crowley, Matt, 138
Crying Jew (horse), 107
Culberson, Victor, 137
Currie, Alex, 138
Curry, Richard, 25
Curtis, Edwin Louis, *115*, 115–16
Curtiss, Charles F., 131
C. Y. Jones (horse), 107

147

Dahlman, James C., 84–85, *85*
Dallas Corn Exposition, 127
Daulton, Henry C., 132
Denny, Arthur Armstrong, 141
Denver and Rio Grande Railroad, 131
DeSmet, Pierre-Jean, 131
Dickenson, James, 25
Dobie, J. Frank, 140
Dodge, Gen. Grenville Mellen, 131
Dorlandt, Lambert, 14, 16, 18, 23
Dubuque Cattle Co., 78
Duster (horse), 107
Dutchess County, N.Y., and origin of cowboy, 14–19, 20–24

Eade, W. C. (Wes), 132
Earp, Wyatt, 7, 93
Edmunds, Newton, 140
Elliott, Verne, 112
Evans, John, 133

Fernander, Henry, 25
Ferriss, John, 26
Festival of Mountain and Plain, 124
Field, Samuel, 25
Five High (horse), 124
Five Minutes to Midnight (horse), 107, 120
Flake, William, 132
Fletcher, Benjamin, 16, 17, 18, 23, 49
Fletcher, George (Kid), *116*, 116–17
Floyd, Calvin W., 134
Flying V Ranch, 73
Follis, James William, 89–90
Ford, Robert Simpson, 59, 59–60
Fowler, Jeremiah, 26
Frantz, Joe B., 3
French, Peter, 139
French and Indian Wars, 17–18

Geronimo, 93

Giannini, Amadeo Peter, 133
Gibson, Hoot, 8
Gilcrease, Thomas, 139
Gilcrease Institute of American History and Art, 139
Goodall, John W., *90*, 90–91
Goodbye Dan (horse), 107
Gooding, Frank R., 134
Goodnight, Charles, 60–61, *61*, 63
Goodnight-Loving Trail, 60, 63
Grant, Bruce, 10
Grant, George, 134
Great Northern Railroad, 131
Grey, Zane, 8

Hale, John D., 140
Haley, John, 134
Hamblin, Jacob, 141
Hamilton, Alexander, 39
Ham What Am (horse), 107
Hancock, Bill, 109
Hannibal and St. Joseph Railroad, 44
Harper, Jesse Claire, 135
Hart, William S., 8
Hashknife Ranch, 80, 92
Hat Ranch, 91
Hell's Angel (horse), 127
Hickok, Wild Bill, 7
Hill, James J., 131
Hill, William, 25
Hinkle, James Fielding, 137
Hitch, James K., *70*, 70
Holdrege, George Ward, 136
Holliday, Cyrus K., 54, 55
Hollister, Col. W. W., 133
Holt, Henry M., 135
Hooker, Col. Henry C., 132
Hoover, Jake, 98
Hough, Emerson, 8, 9, 46, 48
Houston, Sam, 12, 13, 38, 40, 131

HT Ranch, 138
Hudson, Henry, 17
Huntington, Collis Porter, 133

Iliff, John W., 73, 133
Irvine, William C., 85–86
Ivins, Anthony W., 141

JA Ranch, 61
Jeffers, Myron D., *77*, 77
John Clay Banks, 69
Johnson, Ben, 139
Johnson, William, 17, 28
Jones, Buck, 8
Jones, Charles J. (Buffalo), 135
Jones, Dr. L. L., 135
Jones, Tom, *71*, 71
JO Ranch, 136
Judson, Edward Zane Carroll. *See* Buntline, Ned
Jug Cattle Co., 89

Kane, John, 26
Kansas Pacific Railroad, 42, 100
Keith, Morell Case, *72*, 72
Kendrick, John Benjamin, *86*, 86–87
Kenedy, Mifflin, 55, 140
Keogh, Frank, 138
Killhorn, Emil C., 135
King, Capt. Richard, 54–55
King Ranch, 54–55
Kingsbury, Adkin W., 135
Kinkaid, Moses Pierce, 136
Kino, Eusebio Francisco, 132
Kittredge, William, 139
Knight, Jesse, 141
Knight, Pete, 106, *117*, 117–18
Kohrs, Conrad, 61–62, *62*

Lamar, Mirabeau Buonaparte, 12, 38, 40
Lasater, Edward C., 140
Lazy D Ranch, 124
Lemmon, G. E., *73*, 73
Lewis, Mcriwether, 131

148

Light, John W., 78
Linderman, William E., 118–19, *119*
Lossing, Benson, 11
Lote, Mortimer Hewlett, 135
Loving, Oliver, 60, *63*, 63–64
Lucille Mulhall's Congress of Rough Riders, 110
Ludington, Col. Henry, 30
Luna, Solomon, 137
Lytle, John T., 78

Madison Square Garden Rodeo, 113
Manning, Daniel, 138
Maxwell, Lucien B., 137
McCarty, Eddie, 119–20, *120*
McClure, Jake, *121*, 121–22
McCoy, Joseph, 42, 44
McCoy, Joseph P., 135
McCrea, Joel, 8
McDaniel, T. M., 78
McLeod, Charles H., 135
Mears, Otto, 133
Meeker, Nathan, 134
Midnight (horse), 120
Miles, Gen. Nelson, 93
Miller, Henry, 131
Miller Brothers 101 Ranch, 101–2
Mills, B. B., 47
Mitchell, Thomas Edward, 78–79
Mix, Tom, 8, *101*, 101–2
Moffatt, William H., 137
Montana, first ranching in, 47, 60
Moore, Gov., 29
Moore, John Marcellus (Tex), *95*, 95–96
Mores, Marquis de, 91
Morris, Roger, 22
Mossman, Burton C. (Cap), *91*, 91–92
Mulford, Clarence, 8
Munro, Samuel, 21–24, 25–30, 31, 49–50, 103
Myers, John W., 64

NAN Cattle Co., 80
National Cowboy Hall of Fame and Western Heritage Center, 53–56
National Western Stock Show and Rodeo, 109
Nimham, Daniel, 17–19, 20–24, 28, 30, 31–33, 50
Nimham, Jacobus, 22
North, Frank J., 136
Northrup, Moses, 26

O'Donel, Charles M., 137
O–4 Ranch, 76
Oklahoma City, Ok., 54
Oklahoma Strip, 78
One Pound Poctone, 22
Orvis, Dr. Charles Bruce, 133
Owens, Richard Roy, 133

Paddock, David, 25
Palmer, Daniel, 26
Palmer, Gen. William Jackson, 131
Parton, James, 39
Pauly, Peter, 135
Paulding, John, 11
Pawnee Bill Show, 110
Paxton, William A., 136
Payne, David D., 140
Pendleton Roundup, 112, 114, 121
Philip, James, 79, 79–80
Philipse, Adolphe, 16, 18, 22, 23
Philipse, Frederick, 16
Philipse, James, 25
Philipse, Mary, 16
Philipse, Philip, 16–17, 18, 20 ff., 25 ff., 49
Phillips, Fred A., 139
Poole, William D., 135
Porter, Henry M., 134
Post, C. C., 7
Powell, John Wesley, 47
Powers, John Wesley, 134
Prendergast, William, 26, 28
Putnam, Gen. Israel, 30

Raine, William MacLeod, 1, 131
Ranching: beginning of scientific, 75; expansion of, 46 ff.; origin of, 41–45
Remington, Frederic, 8, 131
Revolutionary War, and origin of cowboy, 10, 11, 30–32
Reynolds, Chester A., 53
Rhodes, Eugene Manlove, 96
Richards, Bartlett, 136
Richards, Wilse L., 138
Riggs, Lynn, 139
Roberdo, Coke T., 122
Robbins, Wiley, 74
Robinson, Mrs. Beverly, 16–17, 18, 22, 23, 26
Robinson, Doane, 48
Robinson, Lee, 122–23, *123*
Rockne, Knute, 135
Rodeo(s): cowboys, 106–29; origin of, 104–5
Rodeo Cowboys' Association, 105, 116, 118–19
Rogers, Will, 102, *103*, 103, 109–10, 122
Rombout, Francis, 16, 25, 26
Roosevelt, Theodore, 91, 131
Rothrock, Frank Miles, 141
Ruffner, George C., *92*, 92–93
Russ, Joseph, 133
Russell, Charles, 8, *97*, 97–98
Russell, Hubbard S. Sr., 133
Ruttenber, E. M., 32

Sacajawea, 132
St. Louis Fair, 102
Santa Fe Railroad, 54
Schreiner, Charles A., 140
Scorup, John A., 141
Sequoyah, 139
Settlers' Revolt, 24, 25 ff.
73 Ranch, 80
Shawnee Trail, 63

149

Sheepshead Bay Rodeo, 127
Shreiner, Charles, 78
Sieben, Henry, 135
Siringo, Charles, 8
Slaughter, John H., 93
Smith, Hiram F. (Okanogan), 141
Smith, James, 10, 11
Smith, Jedediah Strong, 54, 55
Smith, Melancthon, 30
Snipes, Benjamin E., 141
Snyder brothers, 67
Sons of Liberty, 27–28, 30, 49
South Dakota, first ranching in, 47
Sowder, Martin T., 124
Spalding, Asa, 27–28, 33
Sparks, John, 137
Spear, Willis M., 142
Splawn, Andrew J., 141
Springer, Charles, 137
Stamp Act, 27
Standing Rock Reservation, 73
Steamboat (horse), 120
Stevens, Isaac Ingalls, 141
Stewart, William Morris, 137
Stickney, Dr. Victor H., 138
Stock Growers' Bank, 69
Story, Nelson, 47, 57
Stratton, Winfield S., 134
Strickland, Hugh, 124–25, *125*
Strickland, Mabel Delong, 124–25
Stroud, William Leonard, *126*, 126–27

Stuart, Granville, 135
Survant, John, 87
Swan, Alexander H., 132
Swartout, Abraham, 30
Swartout, Samuel, 39, 40, 49
Sybrandt, Jan, 14, 16, 18, 23

Taylor, Zachary, 55
T-Diamond Ranch, 102
terBoss, Jacobus, 22, 24
Terrett, William Wiseham, 136
Texas: cowboys of, 11–13, 36–40, 41 ff.; origin of ranching in, 41–45
Texas Jack's Wild West Show, 113
Texas Revolution, 40
Thatcher, Mahlon Daniel, 134
Thode, Earl, 106
Three Sevens Ranch, 90
Tilghman, William M., 139
Tinhorn Rebellion, 31
Tompkins, Charles Harland, *102*, 102–3
Tompkins, Elijah, 25
Tompkins, John, 25
Truan, Fritz, 127–28, *128*
Turner, Frederick, 33

Union Pacific Railroad, 72
U.S. Rodeo Team, 129

Van Courtland family, 25, 26, 28
vanTassell, John, 25
VanWart, Isaac, 11
Voigt, Andrew, 138

Waggoner, Daniel, 65
Wallace, Benjamin Franklin, 80
Wallace, "80 John," 49
Wappinger Indians, 14, 17–19, 20 ff., 25 ff., 31–33
"War of the Outbreak," 140
Warren, Francis E., 142
Waters Cattle Co., 80
Wayne, John, 8
Webster, Daniel, 48
Weed, Benjamin, 26
Western Ranches, Ltd., 69
Western Trail, 63
Wheeler, Daniel Clay, *81*, 81
Whitcomb, Eilas W., 66
White, James Taylor, 41
White, Owen, 13
Wilcox, Stephen, 26
Wilkinson, Gen. James, 39–40, 49
Williams, David, 11
Wilson, Alexander, 34
Wister, Owen, 8
Worcester, Samuel Austin, 139
W. S. Ranch, 76
Wyoming, first ranching in, 47, 66
Wyoming Stock Growers' Association, 87

Yellow Barn Ranch, 77
Young, Brigham, 132

Zumwalt, Oral Harris, 128–29, *129*